A Church with Issues, Tissues and Sunday Morning Rituals

Worship, Survival and Revival "Among the Sistahs and The Brothahs"

written by
Bertha Carson-King

Bertha Carson-King
Bertha Carson-King Ministries
P.O. Box 8689
Benton Harbor, MI 49022
email: kingb0077@att.net

authorHOUSE®

AuthorHouse™
1663 Liberty Drive, Suite 200
Bloomington, IN 47403
www.authorhouse.com
Phone: 1-800-839-8640

First published by AuthorHouse 6/11/2008

ISBN: 978-1-4343-3099-4 (sc)

Printed in the United States of America
Bloomington, Indiana

This book is printed on acid-free paper.

Acknowledgements

To my extended family and friends, thank you for your ever continuing love, support, and prayers as you have touched my life in so many ways. To my friend and husband, Otis King, for your patience as I used some of your quiet time to write. To my daughters, Tara Green and Kimberly King, who support me so faithfully--To my sister, Dorothy Carson-Anderson, who passed away in 2002 after my first book, and who also gave me inspiration and unconditional love as I worked to complete this book--To my other brothers, sisters, friends, in-laws and church members for your prayers, inspiration, kind words and thoughts--To my spiritual sister and friend Bobbie Evans for your help and support in putting this book into black ink. We had wonderful conversations that evolved when we got together on those early mornings and late evenings as a result of me writing this story. Last, but not least, to you my supporters for your continued reinforcement and encouragement of my writing. I thank you and I love you!

Preface

God knows that I love Him more than life itself, but going to church is no joke. According to the dictionary, church is defined as: a formal name of a building, a congregation or a denomination which allows for varied opinions and stresses freedom of interpretation based on the historic conviction, that there is no creed but Christ and no saving doctrines except those of the New Testament.

Jesus said to Peter in Matthew 16:18, "I say to you that you are Peter, and on this rock I will build my church and the gates of hell shall not prevail against it." Acts 2:47 says, "Praising God and having favor with all the people and the Lord added to the church daily those who were being saved." And finally, Ephesians 5:27, completes my defining thought of church, "that He might present her to Himself a glorious church, not having a spot or wrinkle or any such thing, but that she should be holy and without blemish."

We are admonished, to keep an eye on the source, but that is hard to do in a church where there's drama with the mamas and talking that keeps the daddies walking. It's not easy to believe in the power of prayer when some folks just don't care. Where do you go when you go to church looking for strength and leave weak and discouraged? Where do you go when you're lonely and looking for love in a spirit-filled place, but find that a street mentality and sin of the highest order has invaded God's church? Where do you go when trust and deceit creates chaos and jealousy among the sisters and the brethren? It is difficult to be strong when you are committed to go on the most talked about journey in the world...a spiritual life in Christ Jesus.

One day I did some soul searching and I discovered that I was mad. As a matter of fact, I've been mad for a long time. I've been mad at my parents, mad at my relationship with my ex-husband, mad at my career and mad at just about everything.

I didn't get answers to my prayers, and my circumstances did not include divine guidance to pull me through. However, when I went to church, I knew how to play the "how are you doing, I'm fine game" with a smile.

I am motivated enough to change negatives for positives, because I know that many of us lose opportunities and miss blessed possibilities. Also, realizations emerged of self-fulfilling prophecies and self-defeating ideologies promoted from within. In a nutshell, I am my own worst enemy! I'm tired of playing this game of life which gives me few intrinsic rewards. It is time to sow some seeds of joy and hope. Some seeds of love and peace, prosperity and abundance--seeds of healing and deliverance. I've decided that there will be no captives, no bondages on this journey. There will not be a white flag of surrender, although retreat is always an option to plan future strategies. It is time to explore and taste the fullness of God's love. It is time for me and other children of God to examine our theology so that we are not blown away by every seminar, personality and doctrine. It is time for men and women of Christianity to close the numerous denominational and gender gaps so that we can grow together.

One of my most prized possessions is my soul. There are valuable lessons to be learned from family drama whether at home or in the church. I cannot afford to lose every battle or moan through every crisis and give strength to every rumor. Real soldiers in God's army must rise to a higher calling, a higher level of commitment than the average person on the street. If you give in to hatred, criticism, sarcasm and endless confrontations, you will ultimately destroy yourself. There is hope for you and me, as well as for those that we love.

There is hope for the alcoholics, drug addicts, mentally impaired, the homeless and jobless, the atheist, the spiritually bankrupt, the liars, the cheaters and the sick and lonely as well. There is a unique, awesome and loving Savior, who can heal all conditions and deal with all concerns.

It is up to you to discover within yourself the means to lift your spirit and calm your mind. When I need a word to encourage my burdened heart, I turn to God and literally ask Him for a "Word." I tell Him, "Lord, I need a word from you. I cannot make it through these storms without your support and guidance."

You ask me why I love Jesus Christ. I love Him because my Father in heaven answers me and gives me a word, regardless of the hour. I always know His voice, His assurance and His discipline. I know it because it is aligned with my request. Come with me through the jungles of a ripe harvest with few laborers. See as I do the stresses, the human entanglements, the sufferings, heartaches and triumphs of the sanctified, but less than satisfied, members of many denominations. Allow me to give you something to talk about, something real and of substance. Something people whisper about, but fail to acknowledge for fear of retribution, alienation or criticism. Are you a woman with many characters and facets to your life?

Do you look for the obvious, then groan and moan for the mystique? There are impressive victories in knowing who you are in Christ, in knowing your purpose and goals to your success. Many of us begin our life long affair with ourselves, drawn from knowledge gained from our mamas and grandmamas. If knowledge is power, then we truly have a lot to learn and many of us need access to an instant action verb to motivate us.

We have wept and rejoiced, often times been grilled and drilled in the art of loving. We exude charisma and portray the magnificent, devastatingly attractive woman of faith. We are women represented as "divas of the gospel" and written about in best selling novels.

Join other women as they continue to grasp the significance of their existence. Be a role model to those who have no evidence of what womanhood entails. What they've seen has created a dichotomy of suspicion and dissension about the whole process. This is a new world, a world that is often harsh—a world that is a bitter pill for those who live in an environment where few people play by the rules. If you see how we preach renewal, revival, restoration, dedication, meditation, sanctification and so much more to unprepared minds, then you will understand why we must pray. Many of us can help them heal in ways that few can, because we've walked in their shoes, and drank from half-filled cups just as they have.

Let's talk about the sisters in the pews with too little food and worn out shoes. Let's remember the brothers who pray with a tune, those who have never been a groom and refuse to stay in the prayer room. Don't forget the members who grieve and very seldom receive a word of encouragement or an offering of love to help him or her to the next level of blessings. Oh yes, we have a charge to keep.

This mission work will never be done, but you know what? We'll be able to count our blessings and sleep at night. We ought never to forget the emotionally disturbed members who are never satisfied, never ready to forgive, never without an excuse to grumble or find fault, never happy and who never have enough of anything. They are the perpetual poor, if not in actuality, then in principle. They steal joy and tranquility from others and lay a claim on the fortunes of the blessed.

These are the ones, the Holy and righteous disturbed saints, who need a psychiatrist, but go to an elder or a pastor who offer everything but what they really need - counseling. Never mind the fact, that the elder or pastor has a private psychiatrist whom he or she visits regularly, after the member in question leaves their office. Don't even ask how many members have left the church because they were confronted about their dress, their lack of social grace, church etiquette or facial make up. So many people harmed by a small majority of discontented saints. Our response and that of leadership is "let's pray for them" or to tell them to "be strong and let God work it out." When what they really need is love, teaching and guidance.

Where do you go when rest seems impossible in the house of God and yet we play the games and call out names to blame and shame? Where can we go as we praise and worship as though we are all the same? God never seems enough, but the word of God let's us know that "He is more than enough." No matter what you are going through, this book will enlighten, encourage, sadden and cause you to laugh when you want to say "wait a minute." You will cry, ask forgiveness, see yourself and others; but, hopefully be motivated to change your attitude and lifestyle towards your fellow Christians. I cannot save anyone, nor does this book take anyone or two people to use as examples. All characters identified in this storyline are figments of my imagination, although African American culture and life experiences certainly play a role. I have allowed the Holy Spirit to direct this project and His purpose has made the wait worthwhile. Go with me to a day in the life of a sister in Christ, who gets caught up in the Sabbath Day drama of the "sistahs and the brothahs."

Chapter One

"Who can find a virtuous woman? For her price is far above rubies (Proverbs 31:10)

My name is Nayrena Disondro Kokomo and I am a woman of faith, willing to stand strong and unafraid to walk into her season. A woman determined to make her life better despite so many disappointments. I can't explain why I am not receiving therapy for the craziness and insane impulses that has often interrupted my life. All that I can surmise is that God has been abundantly and supernaturally good to me.

I am told that there are any number of people; family, friends and church members who have been influenced by me, a woman of God, although few of them really know my story. I was born prematurely in the State of Mississippi to two loving parents, Ezra and Elana Disondro. I grew up in a decent home with seven brothers and sisters. I was a middle child, spoiled and protected, by my older siblings and envied by the younger ones because I created my heaven where I found it.

Education for me was not a challenge. I excelled in math and English and often used my skills to assist family members who had difficulties with their studies. As good as my parents were to us, they did not accept Christianity as a way of life. What they stressed was mother's wit (common-sense knowledge), family commitment and work ethics. Elementary, secondary and college became my measure of success and then I obtained employment with a Fortune 500 company.

One day as I sought for purpose and vision in my life, I met a man, Fred Kokomo, who told me all the things a woman in love would want to hear.

Until then, my life had been consumed with getting an education and living up to the expectation of my parents therefore, I was "ripe for the picking." Oh, this girl knew that a kiss was a kiss, but Lord help me when it came to matters of the heart.

Fred introduced me to "church", religious beliefs and the etiquette associated with it. He explained that unless I became a Christian, he could not have a committed relationship with me. I was invited to visit his church quite often and finally, one Sunday morning, I made up my mind to join. The minister preached a Word that day as he did previously that was foreign to my beliefs and upbringing. However, the powerful message he presented inspired me to study and learn more about the Bible. Even more than the developing relationship with Fred was a love for the riveting sermons that I heard. The Word of God began to take hold and began to live within my soul. Those who knew me said that they observed a new lift in my walk, a new glow on my face and a spirit of love beyond anything that I had ever experienced.

Something is happening to me that I don't understand. It has empowered me to walk in my purpose while acknowledging my faith in an all-knowing God. I am energized by the connection between my biological family and my theological family.

When I look around me and see how good God has been to me there is no turning back--back there in my past is where the pain, the scars, and the suffering resides. I am going forward with few regrets to see the King of Glory who shall wipe away all of my tears. He will know how to rock me in His arms and show me what real love can do to a broken spirit. I can see Him do the "Color Purple" dialogue with me as He lovingly says, "Everything that has been done to you will be returned to those who did it to you and you will be rewarded for your faithfulness. Everything that has been taken from you will be restored according to your request. It is harvest time and it is your season to reap the fruits of your labor."

Whatever this feeling, this joy, this peace, and this awesome moment of solitude – I cannot comprehend the direction of its flow. What I do know is that this is my time to be blessed. I am tired of being a mediocre Christian who just wants to be one in the number. I want to be creative, available, obedient, and holy in my walk with God. I want to know that He knows that I am on the soul winning team of baptized believers – able and capable of speaking, keeping and standing on His Word. I want to stand before man, unashamed of my life and the Gospel that I live by. I want to enter the sanctuary and have those in my presence appreciate me for the love and support that I bring into the service. I want to usher in the presence of the Holy Ghost and know that there is power in my anointing for the Lord is the keeper of my soul.

There is no one who can counteract this feeling because it is intangible and you can't touch the depth of this joy that the world did not, would not, and claimed not to have given me. Oh, I know that there is a "balm in Gilead" that never fails to work on the root of the problem. The issues that destroy and divide us are often so devastating that we sometimes cannot see the tissues of healing, of hope, of love and ministry that will wipe away our tears as tissues do in our moments of distress.

When we put away rituals of religion that bind and shackles our service to God, what a day of rejoicing it will be. Some rituals are necessary in order for us to be servant-oriented and productive. However, when we can see the destructive behaviors that are attached to some of them, it is time for someone to say, "Change of habit is good for the Sabbath." Anyway, this is one of the most exciting, wonderful, and miraculous days to be in the service of God.

I am going to meet personalities who may or may not embrace me, and they should not have to without a revelation to me. I have a greater responsibility to approach them since I received the commission to embrace them. And when the feelings are mutual, we have learned and lived what God wanted to accomplish in the lives of His children. Signs and wonders will follow those who recognize the human spirit and celebrate the spiritual anointing.

You have been allowed to view a capsule view of my life before I came to church today. As I enter the sanctuary, I can already see the drama that inevitably comes with Sabbath worship service. It has nothing to do with faith and praise to God. I can see the dress-ups and the mess-ups; those who are emotionally charged. Then there are those who have been legally and sinfully charged; those who stand on nothing, but desire everything that God has to offer. I see those who are real and those who come for a thrill. I see liars and backbiters; those who hate and those who cannot relate. I see those who love and want to catch the first train for Heaven above, but don't want to die to get there.

There are so many people, just like you and me, who want to be saved and free from the sin and suffering of this world. I like to rhyme because this is my time and my season to shine. I came today for a Word from the Lord that I may be blessed with healing and abundance from my emotional and spiritual deprivation. Jesus does not have to stand at the door and knock. I saw Him coming in the Spirit, heard His voice and opened the door. You see, I have been through too much to leave Him out of my business.

I have come a long ways from yesterday to get to my evolution of today. I crossed through valleys you've only heard about, in order to speak a word of hope to those hurting and throwing up their hands while going to hell by way of the church.

I know the games, the power struggles, the enemies and the victors. I also know, that time says "enough is enough and to get your house in order."

Chapter Two

"So ought men to love their wives as their own bodies. He that loveth his wife loveth himself. (Ephesians 5:28)

If you haven't been to church on a Sunday morning, you haven't really been to a "real live" church. Far be it from me to criticize anybody else's church, I'm talking about my church, The Better than Blessed Rock of Ages Non-Denominational Church. We believe in the fire and the Holy Ghost, the Trinity and God as supreme ruler and organizer. We believe in love and prayer to the Master above. We believe in unity and keeping our sanity. We believe in the gospel of Jesus Christ and that He paid the ultimate price and went on the cross so that our souls would not be lost.

We believe in relationships and endless meal time fellowships. I admit that we have many beliefs, heartaches, griefs, hurts, pains and every kind of issue. We also believe in the poor and the needy, the wealthy and the greedy, but we all come to church regularly on the Sabbath day. I can't speak for your church, but I can tell you about mine.

When Fred asked me to marry him, it was like having the president of the United States rejoice at peace in Iraq. I proudly accepted his proposal in the presence of family and friends. We had a wedding with all the trimmings including a huge wedding reception. I thought on that day that if God had anything better to offer, He would certainly keep it for Himself.

I was responsible for the salvation of some of my siblings because they witnessed the evidence of true faith in my life. No longer did they share the atheist beliefs of my parents.

Actually, I don't think my parents were true atheists, it was just that they had been beaten down by the systems that be and there was no apparent God to take the chains of racism and economic bondage away. It was such a joy to see my family members praising and worshipping God in Spirit and in truth. More than anything, they saw me loving someone who appeared to love me more than life itself and they were happy for me.

I was on top of the mountain, so to speak, and was slow to see my feet slipping. At first, I thought I was imagining the change in my spouse, but it didn't take long for me to wake up. This has become a traditional story for so many people whether in the church or not. My clue did not come until I intercepted a phone call and discovered that my world had turned to dust.

Little lies became big lies and deceit made me retreat. My husband was cheating in the very church he brought me into and in the presence of the Almighty God that we professed to worship. "How could this happen in the House of the Lord?" I cried, "How could he defile the name of God and corrupt the Lord's Kingdom, not to mention the young woman he dealt with? How could this woman smile in my face Sunday after Sunday; call my house regularly, talk about Christ and teach a missionary class? This woman's stated reason for calling Fred so many times was to discuss their church administrative assignments. Naively, I had observed that the meetings they attended became longer and longer. It was only when I innocently learned from one of the other members that no meetings were scheduled at the church during the times they were supposed to be in meetings that I began to suspect the truth.

One day, I received a call from a source that I least expected, from the boyfriend of the woman in question. He called to inform me of the affair, with dates and eye witness accounts of their hotel liaisons.

By then, I already knew most of the gossip and drama associated with their adultery. Knowing the truth about their sinfulness did not prepare me for the emotional pain and hurt I experienced.

The grief cut through my heart like a dull knife. I wanted to die, to commit suicide, wrong though it was. It seemed that my tears would never stop and I was vulnerable, naked and inconsolable. The first thought that occurred to me was to call someone, but who would I call? Who did I dare drop this bomb on, especially when everyone thought Brother and Sister Kokomo had a "perfect marriage," but then again, did they? Maybe I was the only one who didn't know? And that made me feel even worse before the anger set in.

Slowly the pieces of the puzzle came together. The pity looks, the back rubs, the people who approached me lately with words such as "Honey, let the Spirit lead you" or "Men will be men, so we pray" and "You look like you are burdened and the Lord told me to tell you to drop your heavy load". I won't forget the moment when one of the mothers of our church surprised me with this revelation, "Baby, you can't miss what you can't measure. Take it from me, hold your head up and be strong. Pretty much 'cause many a woman in this church building done been where you at now. You better heed what I say and keep what you got. A piece of man is better than no man. Don't throw your breastbone to no heifer out on the farm cause she can't 'preciate what you had to do to bring it home." I was stunned and thoroughly confused. Now you know some of my history and the reasons I don't take church for granted.

I made it to church today, on time, and the drama has already started. Service had not begun, but stuff happens just before the worship takes over. I can hear her now, my best friend, Adrienne Artest, sitting miserably in the pew next to me at church.

She is complaining bitterly about her lonely, but single circumstances of life. "Girl," she said, "look at him, standing there looking like you can lap him up, like a cat lapping cream. I am so tired of his behind. he's happy and content spending my money. This has got to stop. I have been such a fool. Look at that suit, made for a body like his. My money bought that suit for him. I give you permission to look at this pimping brother on the deacon board. Observe how he struts, like he paid a million dollars for every piece." Her voice started to tremble and then I noticed tears running down her face. I reached over and clasped her hands in mine for support. Those around us patted her on the back and fanned her vigorously because the members assumed she was in the spirit of praise and worship.

She and I made eye contact and the humor of the situation did indeed cause us to shed real tears. She whispered, "We'll talk later" and I nodded in agreement, knowing that the man in question, Rudy Rutherford, was going to be nagged to death after church for his actions. My other friend, Glenda Surrell, was the beauty of the group. She stood tall in her stocking feet, 5'10" to be exact, with a figure most women would die for. Glenda reminded me of "Shug" in The Color Purple, because she could care less about an intimate relationship with other women's men nor did she hesitate about being in their presence. She would flirt outrageously without regard to protocol of when, where, who and how much. We love her though, because she is a friend, who will not cross the line of friendship for a sexual encounter. I could tell that Glenda had her "flirt face" on because she was dressed to the nines and smelled of White Diamonds and Cepacol mouth wash.

The object of her affection was Reverend Sean Jamison of the Church of Divine Revelations. He was a guest minister invited to lead the church's revival and recently he had come to visit prior to the revival.

My problem with Reverend Jamison was that he knew or should have known the "ways of the women and the men" and the "birds and the bees." After all he was a married man, three times to be exact. Glenda attacked him like a piranha attacking a human body in the middle of the sea. They asked her to sing a solo and she sang loud and added extra notes in order to gain his attention. What her body and persona did not provide, trust me, her musical skills did. I knew that he was hooked when he looked exclusively at her as he preached about "Temptation That Makes You Want to Run On to See What the End is going to be!"

I felt sorry for his wife, poor Sister Renee Jamison who appeared to die a slow death, as she watched the flirtation between her husband and Glenda. Later, I shook her hand and invited her to join some of us after church, but she declined the offer. I noticed that she had unshed tears in her eyes and observed her hopeless resignation instead of a will to fight with confidence and self esteem. Her pride allowed her to ignore the open behavior of the two offenders of the church covenant, although I knew she missed very little.

This behavior was not unusual to me, because I had seen it many times before. I've seen women smiling while obvious tears stood in their eyes, but their pride would not allow them to fall in the presence of others. Was it my business to observe any of this? No, it wasn't, but frankly, how could anyone not see the drama. You see, for me to see suffering of any kind provokes compassion in my spirit. I always want to rescue the down-trodden in some way, but I've learned to stand back most of the time and pray. The choir kept singing "What God Has for Me, Is For Me," but my unbelief was regrettably telling off on me.

There was time that I was still trying to find "Mr. What God Has for Me," so I could tell sister thang, whoever she happened to be, to stop trying to get ahead of me; that the brother was designed for me.

Everybody I thought I could be with seemed to be in a relationship with someone else. I created a new declaration that was not public, that stated that 'some of these sister girlfriends were going to have to let go and allow someone else to have a turn.' I was still with the name it and claim it group. Miss Thang had her turn and she had to get off her emotional roller coaster, and understand that divine providence was in the plan. I wanted her to let me have my turn. I believed that she read the bible, but evidently she stopped in Numbers and I was in the book of Corinthians. This was a side of me that they didn't see at church – a recovering sinner--still in kindergarten. I know that God is still working on me.

I know you are wondering, which book I was talking about in reference to Miss Thang.. It didn't really matter because she didn't know either. All I knew then was that the book talks about all of us 'belonging to one body and one church.' According to my "Eros" understanding, this man has one body that we both wanted to share in a charitable way. At that time, I did not want anyone shushing me and accusing me of blaspheming the gospel. I was definitely saved and sanctified and definitely not "satisfied." I desperately wanted to re-marry and find a husband like Sister Angela Janae's who loves her to death. I believe that because church rumor has it that he almost killed a man for looking at her. He tells her all the time "I love you honey" and she gives him a look like she done found a new love. That is the kind of love that I want--a love that melts your insides and makes your outsides jump up and testify. He buys her gorgeous clothes and diamonds to die for. And to top it off, he looks like a Denzel clone.

Hallelujah! One day he spoke to me in a tone that caressed my spirit. My blood pressure shot up to 200. Well it seemed like it did!

Sister Janae was no where around and I decided to push the flirt button, so I said in my sexiest voice, "What are your plans for tonight when the chickens go to sleep?" He looked at me with a smile and replied, "At home where roosters ought to be with the butterball chicken of the litter."

I know he didn't just put me down. I was too through! Child, you could have sold me for a nickel. He made me feel so cheap and that made me angry. I didn't believe that he could try to live such a saved life with a fine woman like me tempting him.

Anyway, I think he's got Alzheimer's. Ain't nobody that strong to resist love portion number one. Thank God for truly saving me from my ignorance. When I think of some of my words regarding another woman and somebody else's man, I am so ashamed. The Holy Spirit saved me from myself through His guidance. I was just out of a bad marriage and here I was determined to ruin my life again. What right did I have to blame a woman for wanting to have similar privileges as I, with a man, illicit though it was? And in the House of God to think about sin as if it was second nature to our faith. I was hoping for "big time forgiveness."

Chapter Three

"In the beginning was the Word, and the Word was with God, and the Word was God. (John 1:1)

Oh Lord, here comes Brother Dale Vision. It ought to be a law against a seventy-five year old senior citizen perpetrating a player from the old school. Oh no, he's going over to see Sister Sondra Davis, who looks to be about thirty years old.

It ought to be a law against what he's doing now. He's pulling up his pants in the front as though that will make him taller or make him appear younger. He's got dye in his hair, eyebrows and his mustache. He looks alright, but I know he's used an eyebrow pencil to make some non-existent side burns 'cause they kinda look like Elvis Presley. Poor Sister Davis looks like she is in a panic, nervously shaking her head and backing up to escape his advances. She's looking over at me like she is pleading silently for help. They may have to call the paramedics to revive her if something is not done quickly. And I am always up to the challenge of intervention.

I approached them as Brother Vision was talking loudly to her. The old dude was on a roll. He didn't have his hearing aids on so he had to talk loud. He was saying, "Sister Davis. How you doing? Shore look good to me. I been watching you for weeks and the Lord spoke to my spirit and told me to marry you. Yes he did. He told me to get ready and showed me you in a vision. Pick your date and we'll tie this thang together; strong lak the Lord said it ought to be. I could have picked any one of you gals here at church, but you're the one that caught my eye with that dress you wore last Sunday. I can see that you like nice thangs. I can buy you any dress that you want from Sears or Walmart. They always got a sale going on.

Don't worry 'bout the money. The Lord will provide. I'm getting warm just watching you girl! What day, time and month? Make it soon. Make it real soon! Brother can't wait forever. I ain't got a lot of time lak these young brothers."

Sister Davis just kept shaking her head and saying "no" as though she was having a nightmare and couldn't wake up. He didn't even comprehend or hear what she was desperately trying to say. I felt that I had to intervene for her sake. "Brother Vision," I said, with authority and I meant every word. "Didn't you hear her say no? She already has a man in her life and that's that. See you next Sunday morning. Do you understand?" Brother Vision hesitated and then proceeded to look me up and down like meat on a discount rack. He had the nerve to ask me, "It's none of your business, but if she got somebody, so be it. Since you talking, I been watching you too. Do you have a man? Maybe, you talking 'cause you want to be my woman. Do you want to be with me? Are you jealous of me talking to Sister Davis?" I looked at him as though he had eaten onions and garlic and then rinsed his mouth with chitterling juice. I told him emphatically to get out of my face and find a senior citizen center for his lady of the hour. Needless to say, he smiled and said, "Girl you got a sassy mouth, but I likes you real good so don't wait to long or I'll be taken." He winked at me and strolled off toward the sanctuary. My prayer was that he would be taken as well and disposed of as soon as possible. I told you that God is working on me and he's not through with me yet.

The Sunday drama was getting to be a bit much. The service was good and when it was over, Glenda and Adrienne beckoned me to come over, so that we could go home. Today of all days, I was ready. Shaking hands and smiling at phony people takes a lot of energy out of a person. I felt as though I was literally drained. They, the elite members of the church, labeled me as "superwoman and aggressive." They described Adrienne as, "Ms. Motor Mouth of the south." I lived up to their gossip, but Adrienne didn't deserve her label. She is different… speech impaired. In spite of everything, we love each other and that counts more than what anybody else can say. And I already described Glenda for you.

I have so many thoughts about life and the pain, pleasures, stress and power that it brings. I want to help others become stronger and to appreciate one another more. I've played and been played, strayed and stayed, weighed and obeyed, but I know that there is a God who can save anybody. I must get my life aligned with the Word of God.

I recognize that it was He who saved me when I couldn't identify myself or my purpose. So often we try to please other people rather than ourselves or those faithful to us. I've determined that it is time for me to go beyond friendship in order to be truthful and a Disciple of a resurrected Savior who heals and delivers. I am a woman of many perspectives, many gifts and celebrations, many joys and many sorrows. I have been hallowed and anointed, broken and repaired, by physicians and the Lord. I have been severed from family and friends who have loved me once and hated me twice. I have experienced numerous relationships, which have been developed and cultivated, but few that have sustained the hands of time.

"Why is it?" I ask myself, "Why is it that a person can give and give and others can take without regards to another's happiness?" The Lord responded with an answer:

> *"Trust in me. Lean not on your own understanding. In all your ways, acknowledge me and I will direct your path. (Proverbs 3:5-6)Remember that you have an advocate--One who knows how to comfort and supply all of your desires. It is time for you to move on. It is time for you to stop dwelling on past issues and your own unforgiveness. Love is unlimited and there are no boundaries.*
>
> *Allow me to walk with you through a life of valleys and hills of enlightenment. As I lead you, the journey may not always go towards your desired destination, but walk anyway. The pain may increase, but when you see yourself in unfamiliar territory, pray through the experience because you are not alone. Recognize that others have crossed before you and now you stand as a guide of inspiration to those coming after you. They will be your models of success for they came from private to public victories to be here today. Trust me and prosper."*

Yes, we can laugh now, but back in the day, you know we pulled off our shoes and did the "sister-girl neck thing" and dared anybody to cross the line. We lost our self esteem and self-control back then and unless we have given our hearts to the Lord, we are still losing it. I am still learning to listen for God and His invitation to come into my presence. He won't force His way in, although He is already there. He waits for us to allow Him to enter before He can intercede. It is up to me to stop getting caught up in my "sistah" stress and wait on God to speak to my deliverance.

CHAPTER FOUR

"For I mean not that other men be eased, and ye be burdened: But by equality, that now at this time your abundance may be a supply for their want, that their abundance also may be a supply for your want; that there may be equality:" (II Corinthians 8:13-14)

CAN YOU FIND TRUE LOVE IN THE house of God? I used to say "Yes" but I am a little bit leery lately. Actually, the question is "Who are you going to love and marry?" The choices are too few. And yet, God ordained marriage, therefore, faith has decreed that in the shelter of the Lord, there is a mate for a deserving sister and brother who live under the blood of Jesus. However, there are boundaries that the Lord instituted for us to follow, and to cross them without righteousness as an attachment; will bring destruction and division into the relationship. Even in the House of Prayer, we become cynical about love and marriage. Perhaps, it is because so many homes are in turmoil that people tend to see the grim reaper coming toward them singing "Who is going down to the grave with me?"

There was a middle-aged couple in our church, Brother Eli Cavanaugh and Sister Megan Turner. She was approximately fifty years old and Brother Eli was somewhere between fifty five and sixty years old. They both were widowers and not ready for a love relationship with other people, but they eventually fell in love and their devotion to each other was tangible. You could actually feel the energy and bask in the warmth from their smiles and covert looks at one another. I noticed that Sister Megan started to dress with more distinction as she wore bright and vibrant colors and her coordination of styles were more youthful.

Brother Eli had seemed to have more charisma than ever with a few more clothing that looked somewhat younger. He was as light in features as she was dark. He had gray eyes and a jovial spirit. His humor embraced unbelievers and saints alike. Even in his sadness he would cheer up someone else who was going through some hardships. Mr. Eli didn't really care about name brand suits or shiny Stacey Adams shoes. He had definitely cleaned up for the better in clothing and his physical appearance. He appeared to shave more frequently and was liberal with the cologne.

He does not look his age despite extraordinary experience as a caregiver. His wife died of uterine cancer after twenty nine years of marriage. This blessed man took care of his sick wife and was a wonderful father to their young teenage daughter whom they had late in their marriage. He didn't even ask his family members for help with his responsibilities. When his wife died, you could visually see his grief and pain at her loss. As a single parent, he became the nurturing parent to his daughter by making sure that she received care and love regardless of his work schedule.

Brother Eli never thought that he would have love again until he met Sister Megan. If he ever married again, he wanted a woman who would commit to not only him, but his child as well. In other words, a woman couldn't have one of them without the other. From the time he and Sister Megan began to talk, his daughter was intricately woven into the relationship and the fit was mutually satisfying. Oh, you could tell that they had something that was special and enviable to share with one another. They didn't seem to realize that they were the objects of scrutiny by the membership. What a wonderful, wonderful season to watch their love and know that life is not over until the Lord allows it to be over.

Their love was admirable and taught many of the younger members how to love God's way. They didn't burn in their lust so bad that they had to "Shack up" and taste the fruit before it spoiled or sneak back and forth to spend a few hours in some secret hide-a-way to deceive the church. At their age no one should have taken exception to their relationship, but some critics felt that they were past the point of all that romance stuff and should be monitored to insure that they were "sin free". The rest of the church waited for the gossip that usually came due to drive bys and unannounced drop in visits, but they couldn't find enough evidence to prosecute the two love birds.

As the romance progressed, an engagement ring began to sparkle and one day, the couple privately came to the Pastor and asked him to marry them. He agreed and the entire congregation was invited to the wedding. They chose not to have an extravagant fanfare of a wedding due to both their losses, but I wish you could have seen the beauty of their wedding day. And to top it all off, they went on a cruise ship honeymoon which I'm told was awesome.

The surprise was that brother. Eli invited his two nieces so that they could assist with his daughter who was a part of the honeymoon. According to him, "God joined not just him and Sister Megan, but his daughter too." Then he laughed and said, "But the nights belong to us. We trusted God and He will reward us for our faithfulness." I thought that was really cute.

Another issue that caused tension in our Congregation was the interracial relationship of Brother Rudolph Masters and his white girlfriend named Anissa Dutchmeijer. He moved to our community after being promoted to an executive position with a well known national corporation.

He started visiting the church alone and loved the worship services and decided to join. What he did not know was that the sisters saw this handsome drop dead, gorgeous, brother with bedroom eyes, a voice that caressed you like Barry White and a body similar to the wrestler named "The Rock" as husband material.

We never asked if there was a woman in the picture. Even I had to catch my breath and pray when I saw him. I remember singing an old hymn to myself, "If the Lord Don't Help Me, I Can't stand the Storm. Lord Jesus, Lord Jesus, have mercy on me…" Then I had to let the moment of my season pass. Some of the other women saw him as another conquest sent by God to satisfy their loneliness. The brother could dress. He was like fine wine in the park, in the dark, with Miss Jones. I heard that some women found his number and called the poor brother so much that he changed his number. Then one day, he showed up at church with his soul mate, "the love of his life" as he called her and she was…White. Lord, you would have thought he'd brought a gay lover into the sanctuary. He introduced her as Anissa Dutchmeijer, his future wife. A number of the members stared and whispered among them selves, but treated her respectfully after the initial shock. Sad to say, but after they married, they joined another church where there were more diverse families in the congregation.

Why black women lose out so often to white women in the dating and marriage field is another book entirely devoted to that topic. However, the reality of this day and time is that love has no color. Individuals choose their mates based on love and compatibility. Each woman has to examine herself and determine what she is willing to settle for. It's time for us to stop looking for a man, a husband and wait on the man, whoever he may be, to look for us.

God never stopped speaking life into our situations. His word never changed – we did. We stopped listening and started our own business of "high jacking" to matrimony. Our role in the church is to speak love and show love to those who enter our presence and sanctuary without prejudice.

Chapter Five

"But this I say, He which soweth sparingly shall reap also sparingly; and he which soweth bountifully shall reap also bountifully. (II Corinthians 9:6)

CHURCHES IN THE COMMUNITY, INCLUDING OUR CHURCH, have politicians who come annually to persuade our members to vote for them. One such politician, McHenry Bismotry, is always running for some office in the community or in the state. Whatever it is, it has to be democratic because republicans are all doomed to destruction based on his personal opinion. We listen to the same rhetoric every two to four years from the politicians in our area, especially Mr. Bismotry. He's comes up to the front at Pastor's request and says, "Sisters and brothers. It's me again – your servant of the government and of course, the good Lord. I'm running for (whatever office it is this time), and if you vote for me, I promise to stand by you, the people.

I am going to see that the Government builds new houses, children's centers and better schools. I will personally see to changes being done in this community for my people. You can hold me to my word." The problem is that we do hold him to his word and nothing happens. Also, he says he will stand by us and my concern is that his word is like hot air and standing with him is like standing on sinking sand. My question is "Why isn't he out front, using his position as promised to create better living conditions for his constituents?" He is as slippery as an eel and seems to always justify not doing what his platform defined as critical to his election. After he's finished speaking, we know that we won't see him again until the next election.

I have a response for both democrats and republicans who are currently campaigning. If I don't say this today, it may not be said.

Can I have my day at the podium? "I am an American. I am a woman. An African American woman and proud of it. I attended schools and colleges in the United States of America. As a mother and wife, I appreciate the various cultures that I must interact with in my community as well as around the country.

"Diversity does not frighten me, but some people and their beliefs do. Discrimination and racism has been an umbrella in which I have had to live under, but refuse to stay under in order to achieve my goals. My purpose in speaking out is to express my sorrow at our country's total preoccupation with politics. I realize that politics is necessary and exist in everything that we do and yet, we are human beings with human needs. These needs should take precedence over whether I am a republican or a democrat. As an African American citizen, I refuse to accept the myths, the stereotypes, the dysfunctions and the negativity associated with the black culture. The same belief is attributed to the political generalizations along party lines.

I am tired of the constant bickering and disenfranchisement with any issue coming from either party. It seems that the majority of politicians are afraid to step out of their comfort zones. A political party should not determine what to do when they can clearly see what is right or wrong in a decision. Many of them are fearful to truly stand up and be accountable to all of the people. What concerns me most is that our country is so divided that we have put the United States on hold to examine issues that have no relevance to our growth and development as a country. A few years ago, we put this country on hold in order to deal with the sexual conduct of a president i.e. stains on a dress, political games and scrutiny of the private lives of political husbands and wives.

Don't get me wrong, politicians have an obligation to be accountable for whatever they are doing that hurts this country, however, there are departments in all major branches of government who are designed to handle unbecoming conduct of government officials and they are to bring the results back to the people. This country tried the case before the public rather than deal with the semantics privately before providing the evidence.

Think about it, while we sat before our television sets and discussed and accused Bill Clinton of poor moral conduct as a President, terrorists caught us, in the next election, with our "pants down", planned and killed innocent people. Something has to give in order for our country to prosper and be healed. (11 Chronicles 7:14).

Another thought that comes to mind is that during 911, you didn't hear from any political party, criticism regarding prayer and faith in God. What happened? Even the ACLU was strangely silent about public prayer in schools, courthouses, the White House, and any other setting. What we saw and heard was unity and strength through prayer. As the Twin Towers in New York burned, you could hear from every source on the news "Oh, my God. God help us." Why do you think this was so? It was time for us to stand united and strong in a period of adversity, acknowledging our faith in a sovereign Savior, Jesus Christ, Son of the Almighty God.

I don't condone what President Clinton or any other leader did when leading the American people. They were elected to have integrity, morality, ethics and an expectation that they would participate in legal practices that bring honor to their office and position. If I believe that a politician, regardless of his political persuasion, is a caring and proven proponent of human and civil rights, I vote my conscious. Sometimes that may mean that I am a bi-partisan voter. My personal preference for a governmental body that will make a difference in the lives of the people is more important than which party I am affiliated with.

We ought to be more than a party, more than an organization developed to hate and discriminate against each other so that we can win another election, or another position within the party ranks. Our principles must be on the mission that we have set to take this awesome journey called "life."

I could care less about accolades because I voted Republican or Democrat. I would rather be known as a woman who loved her country – A woman who voted with compassion and truth amidst intense pressure, but without regrets – A woman who saw all men and women as an opportunity to value and respect, no matter the origin or diversity. It is not critical that everyone agrees with me and rally to my point of view. It is important that people stand up and work for peace, hope and righteousness.

It hurts me to know that in the greatest country in the world, we have issues with individuals who are unafraid to express their right to freedom of religion. Am I wrong to remember the constitution and the foundation on which this country was established? Are we wrong to pray and believe the same Bible on which the immigrants accepted as their way of living in this country? Is it not the same Bible that brought them to America in the first place?

I'm talking about a people who came to this country and based their faith on a land where freedom would ring. Am I wrong to say "I pledge allegiance to the flag?" Is it wrong to see religious artifacts as well as every other symbols boldly displayed without malice and persecution? Am I wrong for trying to hold on to what I inherited? If anyone ought to be upset about pledging the allegiance, it ought to be Blacks in American because we are the "only" group who did not come to this country on our own. We came as slaves, chained and bound, to a country that treated us less than animals. Our ancestors had no choice in why they came or how they came.

Therefore, if we can accept the beliefs that this country was founded on, why can't others who don't have the history or the cultural appreciation? At this point in life, I am not overly concerned about the constitution for it was not written for me. As a citizen, I embrace it because it is the best that we have.

I have chosen to live with the portions that unfairly discriminate against my race until they are addressed. If we, as Americans, can accept the beliefs and faith or non-religious practices of other ethnicities, then why can't they accept the principles and beliefs on which this country was founded? If we go to their countries, they tend to live by their religious beliefs.

When folks come to dinner at your house, you don't change the menu unless you know in advance that they are coming.

If you know ahead of time, you discreetly ask their food preference – that's respect. After the dinner is over, you don't necessarily change your menu or method of eating because you had guests. You continue your cultural practice and if you choose to do so, you can incorporate what you learned in the process of eating with others who are different than you. We are flawed in so many ways and yet, when I read and listen to the news media, we are still in a better position than many countries around the world. Titles and positions, though often necessary, limit our exposure to different opportunities. I salute the politicians who are able to cross party lines and not live and breathe the acidity of government, but look to their community for ways to create unity and harmony.

There are times that I am a liberal and at times a conservative. Often times it has nothing to do with government, it's because I'm getting older and wiser. I want to be flexible and accept changes that impact my life and those around me.

Who knows! One day when all of our parties get disgusted, busted or just plain mistrusted – we'll get less stress, greater work and communication from congress and just maybe; those who are weary will want to rest and let the people get the best of their service. That's the way I feel about politics and the people involved in the process of elections. The church is a vehicle for greatness and I suppose that is where I must start. That's right – you heard it from me first.

And as for Mr. Bismotry, I want him to attend church more often so that he is more visible to those who vote for him year after year. Maybe, people will begin to believe and trust in his promises if he becomes the humble servant leader who listens and activates his purpose in the legislative body. I have to be honest with you--he will never get my vote. I know too much about him.

Chapter Six

"Happy is the man that findeth wisdom, and the man that getteth understanding." (I Corinthians 12:4)

On my way out of the church, I hugged a number of members and waved at others. It's time to go because I am hungry and tired. For some reason, I cannot leave this church today. Oh my God, I see Sister Estella Mahohn sitting off to herself with tears streaming down her face. What is going on with her? Is anybody happy in the church? Lord help us! She seems oblivious to the fact that service is over. I took a Kleenex over to her and watched her as she began to wipe away the moisture from her eyes. I hugged her and started to give her another Kleenex that I found in my purse, but she reached out to prevent my efforts and against her will, it seemed, started to talk about her situation. She cried out to me, "I am tired. I am tired of hurting and dealing with the disillusionment of a loveless marriage. I'm tired of pretending to be happy and blessed when I am miserable in a marriage of convenience. I am tired of propping up my man while everybody believes that he is a wonderful provider and a great lover because of his outward show of affection towards me.

Actually, he is cruel outside of the church and rarely shares any of his resources, including his money. This man has also decided not to indulge in sex on any level ever again, while I am expected to accept his decision without question. I am tired of lying on my side of the bed with a man sleeping on the opposite side who wants nothing to do with me."

"We talk about lonely, single women, but I've got a man and I'm still home alone. I can tell you about being married and single at the same time!"

She looked up at me and I'm sure she saw the incredulous expression, bordering on shock, as I tried to digest what I had just heard. I sat there wondering "How can this be? The Mahohn's have the model marriage, or so I thought, with money and a beautiful home. "You are surprised I know," she said, "Most people would be. I have been in denial of my feelings for so long. I didn't want others to feel sorry for me or place judgment on my relationship."

"My husband is pleased at the image that we portray and gives advice to others about marriage and how to be successful, but he doesn't have a clue about what to do with any woman, let alone me. He has the audacity to flirt with other women when I am in need of his affections. He knows that he will not commit physical adultery because he cannot or will not complete the act even with Viagra. I am sorry if I seem too blunt, but I have to release this pain today. I am my husband's testimony to all who know him. They see him through my eyes; what I want them to believe. I validate that he is a master of all things. Sister Nayrena, I go to bed crying and I get up praying, knowing that today is just like any other day."

Needless to say, I was speechless at her revelation. This man that she spoke about, Brother Johnson Mahohn was flawless in his integrity and I valued him from a young woman for his demeanor. Sister Mahohn continued talking as she reached for my Kleenex to wipe her face. "I decided this morning as I watched a television ministry and listened to the sermon, entitled, "You Have Been Set Free By the Blood Of Jesus," that I must deal with my relationship and take responsibility for my own happiness. I am finally willing to stand on my own two feet without waiting to see what others think in order for me to move to my peace of mind. Nobody could have told me that pain of change is a monster.

Why do I think I have to blame somebody else for what is happening in my life? I even want to blame the church leaders because I feel that they should have been able to see beyond the role, the characteristic rhetoric, the persona, and see an opportunity for salvation."

While she talked, I subconsciously watched her hands as she rolled the used Kleenex back and forth in anxious movements. As I glimpsed the beauty of her features with a light foundation of powder and mascara, I think I saw her as never before. Her brown sugar complexion was flawless as were her hair and clothing. The clothing belonged to Jones of New York and she wore each piece as though it were made for a figure from Hollywood. I always believed that she was one seasoned sister who was better than blessed until I listened to her testimony. I had so much compassion for her. She said as though it were an after thought, "I am still young enough to have love and intimacy in my life. Somebody, somewhere, wants to love and be loved by me. I have to get over my anger towards this man who told me that God gave me to him. I have to tell him how I feel."

"I'm going to tell him to go back to God and get a Word or a human repair slip as soon as possible for this girl is about to make serious steps towards the dissolution of this one-sided marital arrangement. I have a husband in name only. A mate who is satisfied to have me bear his name and allow our life to stay the same, but refuses to bear the blame or stop the excuses that seem so lame. Why me? Why have I allowed my self-esteem to suffer the ultimate rejection?" Then she paused, touched my hand in embarrassment, and said, "I'm sorry. I realize that this is a shock to you. I should never have shared my personal business. Please forgive me for my moment of weakness. I suppose I had to release this depression on someone.

I know that I'm next in line for my miracle. I've got to be. God is making a way out of no way and this is my time--my time to be blessed. Surely, my life is not over." Her tears were gone and remarkably, she rose with her usual persona and smile. She thanked me again for listening and I saw her back straighten as she walked out. What could I say? I wanted to say something, but I couldn't find the words in this defining moment of revelation. All I could do was nod my head in farewell and tears began to fall from my eyes. I could not stop them. Sorrow had a new meaning for me. This woman did not deserve to be treated in this manner. I felt such a longing from within, an overwhelming feeling of helplessness. And yet, I was so unworthy to judge anyone with my past history of "hurt and be hurt."

Chapter Seven

"Happy is the man that findeth wisdom, and the man that getteth understanding." (Proverbs 3:13)

Then I heard it. Now, who can this be? Certainly not who I think it is. Yes, it is him in the flesh. "Sister Nayrena, Sister Nayrena, wait a minute." An unwanted voice that I recognized was calling my name. Oh, my God, let me pretend not to hear him and hurry to my car. Darn these high heels that have me limping like a weary cowboy. My mind is telling me to run, but my body won't cooperate. Oh, well, maybe today will be different. I know you wonder who he is. He is Deacon Elroy's son, Damon Elroy. His slow son and I do mean slow! He fancies himself in love with me. He doesn't have a clue about the quality and character of the woman he is pursuing. People have got the nerve to say with a smile, "He has potential. A woman just need to be the head of the house and don't let him talk." Unh, unh, this is too much drama and expectations even for me. A relationship with Damon would cost me too much; my mind, my spirit and my patience. It would be detrimental to him, because when he worked my nerves as he does every time I see him, he would be dead and I would be incarcerated for 1st degree murder.

Get ready, get set, smile and have patience on cue, whew, okay, I'm ready. "Hi, Damon, how are you doing? Praise the Lord for a lovely day." You know I have to keep it real. I'm still on Holy ground. "Where are you going?" I asked. Then he messed up and said, with confidence, mind you, "Over to your house so we can spend time together." Now you remember what I just said about patience? Forget it, the gloves have come off. "Excuse me" I said, with my teeth clenched. "Who on this side of heaven said that you were coming to my house? I know there are loose shells moving around your lighthouse, but you'd better remember who you are talking to."

He looked at me with those big, brown puppy eyes and undaunted admiration. "I love you, Sister Nayrena, with everything I got. You and I belong together. Last night I dreamed about us having four or five children and we both lived happily ever after. Did you have a vision too, cause if you did, it's "on and popping." I don't know what happened, but it seemed like somebody had snatched my breath away. Some words came to me that I thought I could never and would never say. Look at him, standing there, still smiling and looking crazy. "Brother Damon, if you heard a word from God, you would know what is in my heart. The vision I have of you would destroy your very foundation. There will never be a joining together of you and me to produce anything that lives, breathes or speaks beyond the spirit of God. Now take your blessed personality out of my face or I promise that people will discuss how natural you look for years to come. Oh, and another thing, tell your daddy that I am not the one. When you see me coming from now on, get back and get out of my way because I may hurt you. I'll then have to repent and lie down and come before the church asking for forgiveness." Oh no, bad choice of words around him, "lie down." So I added, "Listen man, there is no fire, no smoke, no spark anywhere in my system, so get to stepping." I know that I was wrong, but I crooked my finger at him, symbolizing a gun. I tell you what I learned today...Brother Damon is not as crazy as some folks may think.

When I got through talking and crooking my finger at Damon, he looked at me, screamed in a panic and flew to his father's car. Imagine a forty year old man screaming like a woman. When people turned around to see what happened, I smiled and lovingly remarked about Damon's connection to God and his shouts of praise and adoration. If they didn't believe me, they knew not to say a word.

When I got up this morning, I knew this day would be a difficult one. When your head hurts and you just got up that's a sign. When the hot water in the bathroom fizzles out, that's a big sign. When you look in the refrigerator and there is no breakfast food, that's an awareness sign. When you look at your watch and realize that you are over an hour late for work, that's a huge sign. When the phone rings and you discover that it's your ex-husband, that's a voodoo sign. I knew it and I got up anyway and came to church. I was dressed to kill and mad as the devil.

All I want to do is go home and rest before the afternoon service begins and I keep getting interruptions. Who is that over there trying to get my attention? Oh, it is Sister Sadie Terry. What is she trying to say? "What?" I yelled out to her and she yelled back, "There's food in the fellowship hall," and rolled her eyes up towards the ceiling. "Thank you so much for telling me," I said, "I am so hungry." I followed her to the Fellowship Hall which was on the lower level. I decided to find a seat over by the door, but close to the food. "Sister Terry, this food looks so good. Give me a few greens and… huh, what did you say?" Sister Terry was shaking her head and motioning with her hands for me to avoid the greens. I eased up beside her and quietly asked what was wrong with the greens. "Take my advice," she said, "Child, don't you eat those greens, because they is nasty. I heard that Sister Loraine Blaine cooked 'em and she ain't clean. You know she got that nasty woman's disease and her house ain't clean either." Sister Terry said vehemently, "Why the church let her bring food to these events is beyond me. I just told the Pastor that I would tell her not to bring anymore food, but he advised me to be quiet and let the Lord work it out. You listen to me good. I love my Pastor, but God was working it out when we heard she had issues. My telling her would have been confirmation."

I only heard bits and pieces of Sister Terry's conversation, because I wanted those greens and corn bread. They looked so good, but I could tell that the sister standing before me was not going to move. I looked beyond her as the alleged nasty, diseased woman that Sister Terry described, approached us. She spoke cordially and shook our hands. When I looked at Sister Terry's face, believe it or not, she was a different person. She had a smile on her face and loving words poured from her lips. Sister Terry all but gushed out her charm as she said, "Sister Blaine, you are such a blessing to our congregation. I was just telling Sister Nayrena about the delicious greens you prepared. We need more members like you. How do you feel dear? I know you've been sick for sometime now." Sister Blaine thanked her for her concern and turned to walk away. Instead she came back to stand directly in front of Sister

Terry. Sister Terry backed away in surprise at her actions. Sister Blaine said angrily, "I know what you have been saying about me. I want you to know that the rumors that you have spread about me are a lie. My nasty woman's disease, as you described it, is stage four cervical cancer as well as other health related issues."

"The doctor's tell me that I am terminally ill, albeit in good shape, considering the alternative. I came to this church, because I wanted to receive hope and comfort during a crucial time in my life. I reached out to you and others and I even tried to get involved in the women's group, but few of you accepted me. You have avoided my presence the entire time that I have been here."

"For the longest time, I thought it was me, but I can see now that I am the saved one. I love the Lord and all of you in here, and there is nothing that you can do about it. I no longer care whether you accept me or not. I pray that other converts and new members will be treated with greater love and appreciation than I have received."

She said with visible hurt and pain, "Part of my pain is that there are members of the church who believe your gossip rather than getting to know me personally. Not one of you have called me, invited me over to your home, visited me in the hospital or spoken to me beyond a hello or good-bye. I often think of the song 'What does it cost to carry the cross of salvation? Who do I have to be? How do I have to walk?' Sister Terry, what have I done to you that you would destroy my name and deny me fellowship and love? I pray that you both have a blessed day. Sister Nayrena, I'm sorry that we didn't get to know one another better. I heard that you were a true saint and I hope that what they say is true." Proudly holding her head high, she composed herself and she left through the side door. Once again, I witnessed tears of hurt and frustration.

Oh my God, there are so many hurting people in God's house. I wonder how many people I've hurt along the way. Gossip is destructive and it doesn't care who gets hurt in the process. As I turned to look at Sister Terry, she silently stood there and appeared to be devastated for her part in the plot to verbally assassinate this woman of God. She finally spoke, to no one in particular, in a contrite and hushed tone, "I am so sorry for believing the rumors I've heard and passing misinformation around. Sister Thomas told me and she got it from somebody else. I pray that God will forgive me for my part in Sister Blaine's heartache. I believed what others told me and repeated it without facts. Had we known the truth, it would have allowed us to give her more love and support rather than have suspicion and animosity towards her. I pray that the Lord will give us a second chance to be a friend to her."

How sad, I thought, that we profess to be saved and healed of our sins and yet, we hurt others with our sanctimonious gossip and attitudes. It was not her responsibility to tell us anything about her condition and we still should have loved her. I suppose I am guilty too.

Chapter Eight

"The Lord is my strength and song, and He is my salvation: He is my God, and I will prepare Him a habitation; my father's God, and I will exalt Him." (Exodus 15:2)

It's time for me to go home and rest from this stressed Sabbath Day until service convenes this afternoon. Whew, what a long day. Reverend really preached a powerful message. But what did he say? It was so good, so motivational, but I can't remember the title. He wasn't talking to me specifically, so I guess those who were affected deeply will remember every word. You also know, that some folk won't be at church the next Sunday, because they will still be mad at Pastor for his message. Can you believe that folks still want to drink milk in the Lord's house instead of eating good Angus beef? They hate the truth, but thrive on assumptions and falsehoods. We are to give praise of God's glory, but you may not know it unless you know the Word of God. In spite of the questions you may have about the message or the saints in the church, remember that judgment brings judgment. We are a people who cannot stand to be chastised for any reason. Of course, it doesn't feel good, although the results are usually a blessing because you tend to grow from the positive aspects of the knowledge. A lot has to do with the messenger, whether it is in the form of family, friend, coach, leader, pastor or layman. Their approach and manner will determine the feedback as well as the transfer of information.

I believe that everyone has a dream whether they acknowledge it or not. It seems that almost everybody is talking about what is missing in their lives and what is going wrong. As a matter of fact, you seldom hear people discussing the beautiful life they live with their mates and their families.

Even in some religious arenas, the messages delivered have few examples of saved lives according to the Word of God; therefore, the relevance of the praise service is lost to many parishioners. Now, don't get me wrong, you do see people stand up in congregations and declare that they love according to the commandments. They strongly speak up about love being a wonderful thing, but I dare you to follow many of them out of the church edifice. Their lives beyond the Sabbath speak a different language and they walk with other gods.

There are times when I whisper a prayer for those who are going through problems and heartaches on a number of levels. I pray for God to reach beyond Heaven and provide them with peace, deliverance and abundance. In the depth of my heart, I believe that God hears us when we are advocating blessings for those we love or lifting up intercessory prayers for individuals that the Lord directs us to encourage. He makes the connection through the Holy Spirit and designs with us our own method of response. When I see the results, I don't question whether my prayer got "priority clearance." I simply expect that He can do what He promised. In the book of (John 14:14), God says, "Ask anything in my name and I will do it." And the uniqueness of faith is that He does; which provides glory and honor to His name.

I for one can truly say that I am not afraid to ask God for anything. We have to understand that there is a formula for Saints of God. We reverse the order of our request for blessings. When we as Christians need a loan, we will go to see the banker. When we need food, we go to the grocery store. When we need shelter, we go from realtor or rental agency or to the Emergency Shelter in a crisis. When we need a job, we go to the employment agency. When we need healthcare, where do we go? We go to the doctor's office or the hospital. God is usually our last resource.

There is nothing wrong with going to agencies, that is why they are available to us, however, our first step should be to the storehouse of the Master who created all things and owns everything. It would make sense that we seek the One who is able to supply all of our needs and wants.

We still don't understand that our source is not in what man can provide, but in our Father in Heaven, who owns everything. Everyone who we seek to give us a blessing has a need of their own and as humans, they must go to the same God. He has the abundance storehouse of blessings that we desire and we should not fail to go to the source of that supply. (Philippians 4:19)

What gets us into predicaments is that we have learned to listen to small-minded people who tell us that it's wrong to bother God constantly with requests. They tell us that we should be satisfied with mediocrity and that maybe we are denied our blessings based on some act of reciprocity. I have come to the conclusion that I have a right to ask my God, and yes, I made it personal, "My God" for anything and believe that He will deliver it to me on time. If He said "Ask," I'm not going to walk around pretending that my hands are tied and nobody cares. I have issues with faith like that. There is deliverance in knowing that I have the freedom to ask for what I desire, whether He decides to give it to me or not.

My God is a living, breathing Spirit, who knows my ups and my downs. He created me from the top of my head to the depth of my soul and I refuse to believe that He wants me to suffer for He is my Daddy. My Daddy (God) is rich in whatever resources and privileges we desire.

Others with "Stuff" have turned me down, time and time again, and it was only at the urging of the Holy Spirit that I sought the Lord and He taught me to listen and obey His voice.

I am a new me since I found the Savior. I knew Him and thought I was in His presence, but when I truly recognized His power, the outpouring has been worth it all. Oftentimes, I think of the elders, apostles, bishops, evangelists, pastors and church counselors who deal with issues that are emotionally, psychologically, physically and mentally challenging. Perhaps the reason is because of the number of troubled parishioners and unbelievers constantly coming to them for prayer and consultation. Usually these individuals don't have a personal life of faith even though many of them attend church regularly.

There are a number of hurting people who enter sanctuaries of God looking for a miracle or an answer to their life long dilemmas. Let's face facts. There are issues in the church. Lonely women and men are seeking relationships, especially women, and that may not always mean companionship. Some of them simply want a sexual encounter which signifies the thrill of the chase or to fulfill the whim of a mid-life crisis.

Unless leaders, spiritually called ministers of God, are strong and disciplined, they, too, are ripe for the harvest of forbidden fruit. Satan tells us a great number of lies to entice us into his world of darkness and deceit. And then he stands back to laugh at the demise of Saints who profess to be servant leaders.

Sincere and true leaders of the cloth know that to go into certain areas of temptation will divide, destroy and affect Kingdom building which they have been called to do and yet, they fall. How can they fall, you say, with God on their side? The truth is that they are human and sometimes they lose their vision and power when they are distracted from the presence and purpose of God.

There are members who call the pastor if the dog runs away, if their husbands fail to say "Good morning," or if their child has been disobedient. They call the pastor and his wife if Sister So and So did not put their name on the program and they believe that it was done maliciously. Heaven forbid that their offering was not recognized before the congregation on the Pastor's Anniversary--so much to do about nothing!

It can be 2:00 a.m. in the morning and Sister Pearlina Mae Peartree can't sleep, so she calls the pastor to pray for her situation which will allow her to sleep better. Never mind that the pastor can no longer get his sleep. Then don't forget the calls from the police department that commands the pastor to get up and contact the church financial committee in order to get a member's child, a member or administrator out of jail because they got in "A little trouble with the law." Come on now, let's be for real. We have to pray daily in order to be fulfilled. Glossing over the issue to satisfy the majority of worshippers will not be a cure-all for the wounded minority. There are grieving leaders as well as members. It is time to deal with the chosen few from the pulpit to the back row pews. We have a right to call the pastor when our lives are going crazy, but not to make his or her life crazy.

Chapter Nine

"For whom the Lord loveth He correcteth; even as a father the son in who he delighteth." (Proverbs 3:12)

WAIT A MINUTE. THAT LOOKS LIKE SISTER Susie Aims's daughter, Cherry, over there in the corner with Lonzo Conner's boy, Jerrod. Lord have mercy! I know she didn't do what I thought she did in this church! This is the fellowship hall, but it is still a holy place. Let me tell you about this young, "floor heater," with her dress up to the question mark, and her hair bunched up on her head looking like Patty La Belle in that singing group, before she discovered that somebody loved her. You would think her mama would observe what's going on? The child's got makeup all over her face like a mask. Where is her mama? I just remembered that this is her day for kitchen duty, and she has no idea what is going on with her children.

The woman's got six children, but this one is the oldest and the hottest. Cherry is fourteen going on twenty-five. She what? No, she didn't. She just kissed that boy on the mouth and they're moving closer together. I've got to act fast or we'll be adding another baby to the nursery in nine months. "Cherry," I said sharply to her. "If you don't cut that mess out right now and you know what I mean; I'll beat you down before they dial 9-1-1." Now ya'll don't get me wrong. I love teenagers, but this one seems to strike a nerve with her grown behavior. Look at her, five feet tall and tough as a piece of leather: standing there, rolling her eyes at me, without saying a word. Looking at me like I'm dumb, she sarcastically replied, "What is it, Sister Nayrena? Did you want something? I'm busy at the moment." Then she called to Jerrod, pleading; with her hand on his arm as though I was not there, "Don't leave Jerrod, we've got things to talk about." Poor little Jerrod, he was hot and bothered from the kiss and my interruption. He said, with resignation, "I'm sorry Cherry. I, I… have to be home, to get dinner ready, by the time mama gets off work."

"My daddy has to leave to sing with the male chorus in Lomax today, but I'll see you at school tomorrow. Bye Miss Nayrena." Before Cherry could say anything else, he escaped by practically running out of the door. Cherry turned to me with an accusing expression on her face. She started to say something, but thought better of it. I'm glad she thought about respecting me because I was going to drop kick her in the name of Jesus, and wait on the rest of her family members.

I didn't hesitate to speak my mind. I said, "Cherry, I saw you kiss that boy in an inappropriate manner for a girl your age. Where is your home training? If I ever catch you doing that again, you are going before the pastor and your parents. Any respectful young lady would dress and act like she's decent and value her reputation." I stopped to see if what I was saying had any impact on her. What I noticed was that all the while I was talking this child was looking at me as though I had two heads and a forked tail. If I was scared this would have been a chilling experience.

I continued to speak to her hoping to reach her somewhere between sin and salvation. Her bristling response to me when I finished was "Who appointed you my legal guardian? Who told you that I cared about what my parents or anyone else thinks about my clothing or my behavior. I don't need a babysitter and neither does Jerrod.

As long as our parents are not complaining, why should you care? You old biddies at this church need to take care of your own, business and let the young people be in charge. I'll thank you to mind your own business and I'll see you on Sunday morning…if I decide to come."

I gasped in shock and shook my head in disbelief. Then I went into overdrive without prayer and supplication. "How dare you talk to me in that tone of voice young lady," I warned. "Your little behind need a Nayrena massage and if you say one more word, I'll nail your fast mouth on the cross and crucify it before the sun goes down. Now you can talk to other members like they're your children, but I'll step on you and dance the Cha-Cha on your hot little behind. When I see your mama, I've got some words for her, letting you go running around looking like a hoochie mama.

You can identify with the ones who stand on the corner, I'm sure. And you can pull that one-inch skirt down and while you are at it: get your sexual hormones down to zero, because you are too young to be on the loose with that profane mouth. Yeah, I said it and I can back up every word."

I think I scared the poor child so much that tears ran down her face and she kept saying, "I'm sorry, please don't tell my mother. I didn't mean to disrespect you. I promise not to do it again." I really wasn't going to tell her mother as long as she shut-up and cleaned up her behavior, but I wasn't going to tell her that. I know that I can be tough as anyone on the street, although, I don't like to go there. After all, I am college educated. I never forget my southern culture. The last I saw of Cherry, she was running like a buck deer to find her mother. What I do know is that she won't have a heart to heart confrontation with Sister Kokomo ever again.

I don't know why I am meeting so many dysfunctional Saints today. I already have my own issues to deal with. Lord, anoint them with your Holy Spirit, I pray: for today, I have so little power and patience to deal with other folks issues whether they are male or female. The food smells so good and I have to eat something after all of the drama I've been through.

It is getting late and I can't deal with another person: not another one; not today. But you guessed it—coming up from nowhere is Reverend Aaron Santana. You have to have faith in order to talk to Reverend Santana. He's middle aged, attractive, tall, dark and exceptionally talented, but the man cannot preach. He's got the hoop, and the holler; but no substance. He thinks he's got it, but on the Sundays when he's going to preach, the membership attendance is noticeably smaller. It is so pathetic, because he'll tell everyone in sight, "I've got a message off the hook for ya'll today" and that seals his fate. Members keep wondering when the "off the hook" message is coming. His poor wife sits there as he preaches saying, "Lord, have mercy on him. Give him a Word. Lord, you promised me the last time you would bless him. What happened?" Invariably, someone would whisper to her that others were listening and ask her to be quiet; in a nice way, of course.

Getting back to Reverend Santana here is an example of one of his sermons:

> *"Lord, I pray for those who have sinned as I have on a number of occasions. I pray for God to be merciful. Many of you are not saved because I saw what you did last night. You were in places where you know you didn't belong; and you saw things you weren't supposed to see. I know because I was there too. I was out of order, messed up. Lust had me bound and I cried out in my suffering, "Lord, Jesus, Lord Jesus, help the body that is going astray. I looked upon a woman and lusted after her. Help me Lord". Come somebody, I need a witness, who has been there in the valley of Sodom and Gomorrah with me. I told my wife to look to the hills, and get strength, because I need an anointing. Reverend Jamison, can I get an Amen? You been in many fiery places in your own addiction, am I right about it?" Now you should have been there to see the look of horror on Reverend Jamison's face as he appeared to hold his chest and murmur unintelligible words out loud. He just waved his hand, as if to say, "I give up." Reverend Santana never noticed what was going on. He was on a roll in Babylon country.*
>
> *He continued, "Who is it that sinned before us? It was David who sinned and had another man killed to get his wife. Two of the greatest ball players in history, Michael Jordan and Kobe Bryant confessed to sinning. Well, I got to be fair, a lot of those boys with fame and fortune get caught up in temptation and can't let it go until they run smack into trouble—lose all those big contracts. Jim Bakker, Rev. Jesse Jackson, and other famous preachers*

sinned, and so did Deacon Smith. Well, I don' t know for sure about Deacon Smith, but I heard talk. God told me to tell this entire church to stop talking so much about other folks business and concentrate on your own. I don't talk as much as some people, therefore I will close on this note: Love for God's people brought me here to this moment.

If loving you is wrong, then I must do the right thing. Love has brought a lot of good folks down; and no matter how good they felt, they had to come down. Sister Mariana, you know about that, don't you; with your fine self? My wife, bless her heart, used to be too hot to trot, but God saved her and I won the prize. She gained a little weight, but she ain't bad, no sir. She still got it. After this message, I know somebody out there can't wait to come up and join the church. Whatever you have done in your life, remember that some of us did it before you. There is no reason to be ashamed.

Come on down and take your burdens to the Lord. That way; when you are tempted, you got a shelter; a fence all around you. You gonna sin. It's in the book; but you can be forgiven. All of us here today can stand because we have been forgiven. Thank you for the opportunity and thank ya'll for listening. Be blessed until the next time I preach. Oh, by the way: I'm preaching again over at Reverend Fisher's church on Sunday night at 7:00 p.m. Until then, don't sin. Amen!"

Even with my telling you this, you had to be there to get the full effect. I felt so sorry for his wife. Maybe she ought to start preaching or teaching, it can't be any worse than what he does. When Reverend Santana said, "Hello Sister Nayrena," I quickly responded with a few choice words, and they were curt, "Goodbye Reverend Santana" and walked away. I don't mess around with ignorance. I would not lie and tell him how great his sermon was that day or any other day. Actually, I didn't think anyone got one single, solitary thing, out of that message: except to avoid him more, acknowledge sin, and say as little as possible in his presence, lest they hear it over the pulpit. I know. I know I need prayer. God is not through with me yet. He is still working on me.

My friend Glenda, who is beckoning me to come to her, definitely needs prayer. I thought she had left the premises.

She is vigorously shaking her head and waving her hands at me, so that I can wait for her. I can tell that she is out of breath and angry as all get out as she caught up to me. Without preamble, she said, "How long have you known me, five to ten years, or has it been twenty? It really doesn't matter. That skinny, lying, no dressing, homely, jealous hearted wife of Brother Harper accused me of looking at him too often, and desiring to commit adultery with him. I'm so mad. Of all the men at this church that I can have with a little effort, she thinks I want him of all people." When she paused to take a breath, I questioned her to determine what happened. "What did you say to her? Did others hear the conversation? Are you sure that she was accusing you? Calm down and let's talk about it."

"Of course," Glenda bitterly replied, "Others were watching and heard everything. Then she had the nerve to apologize, but you know my reputation is shot because those listening started whispering and smiling as though they were happy. I may get a lot of attention, and I do flirt sometimes, but it's harmless. It's not my fault that I am beautiful with a figure that women would die for and men can't resist. I guess I'm a magnet for their gossip and jealousy. I may never come back to this church again!" I could not help grinning as the dramatic monologue ended. Glenda looked at me suspiciously, "I see you struggling not to laugh. This is serious Nayrena. I need your understanding and support." At this point, I lost it and laughed until tears ran down my face. She stood there glowering at me and said, "What is so funny?" "Well, first of all," I replied, as I used the table napkin to wipe my face. "This is one of how many times that you've been confronted in this church about a man that you don't care about; and are not attracted to, but whom you flirted with? Girl, when will you learn? You have got to respect a man's wife, and ignore your basic tendencies to get attention. Another thing, Glenda, every man don't want you for your beauty or your intelligence. At your age, you should have learned that by now. They will have your body for a brief period of time, and will leave you at the alter praying for repentance. Move on and learn from this experience. You know that you are satisfied being single and free, therefore, you had better stop preying on homely, tired, and seemingly neglected married men. I'm using your version of the ones you attract. Now, go wash your face with cold water and stop complaining and let's get ready for afternoon service, okay?" There you see it...another episode on this Sabbath to contend with. Where is God? Is He out to lunch or sleeping on one of His heavenly mattresses? Did He forget about me? I just want to know if I am next in line for my miracle.

Chapter Ten

"Children, obey your parents in the all this; for this is well pleasing unto the Lord." (Colossians 3:20).

"Hi, Grandma Edmonds," I waved and she waved back to me. It is so good to see Grandma Edmonds. I didn't know she was here today. I love Grandma Edmonds. She is a great mother of the church--one who believes in the power of the Almighty God. There she is now; sitting with some of the other mothers on the Mother's Board seats. She is short in stature, although she stands tall with us. She has gray hair and is so stylish in her dress, despite her age.

Something else I love about her is her ability to make everyone else feel comfortable and special. You can be having the worst day of your life and a moment in Mother Edmonds' presence will warm and energize your spirit. She promotes love like Jesus, giving out the fish and five loaves of bread. God had to design this mother by request of the angels. Mother Edmonds will tell you about yourself in such a nice way unless you want the whole truth without the preservatives. She has no problems with advising you with "unbuttered" love. Her gift of communication and self confidence are phenomenal.

For example, she told Sister Anna, that she was too pretty and talented to wear so much rouge and lipstick on her face. She said gently, "Baby, you a member of the usher board and you are so pretty and gifted that God is going to bless you for being obedient, and mindful of your greatness. Now do your Mama a favor, and clean some of that lipstick and that red stuff off of your face and start over with less strokes, alright? God is taking your required moderations and teaching you to be a saved and proper young woman. You have a ways to go, but you are getting there. Girl, you have that natural beauty that don't need much. I'm here to help you get your blessings, alright? You can kiss Mama on her cheek when you get back." Now that's what I'm talking about, a woman of wisdom.

It was so funny: the day Mother Edmonds had a life changing discussion with Brother Vision. He was all up in the young women's faces, acting like he was Puff Daddy or somebody close to him; but smelling like Ben Gay. This particular Sunday, he had on a red suit with red socks; and shoes, a red hat, red trimmed glasses, and believe it or not: a red top coat. It was too much, too soon, on one person. Mother Edmonds stood back and looked at him. I saw her pull her glasses off, wipe them off with her white fringed handkerchief, and put them back on again. "Brother Vision, both you and Reverend Sandusky, come over here for a moment. I need a word with both of you," Mother Edmonds said firmly and with authority. Then she targeted Brother Vision and held up her hand before he could protest, and said, "Brother Vision, if you don't remember your age, let me remind you. You are a senior citizen: not too much younger than I am. What in the world are you looking for? Ain't no woman; and I do mean, not a one, is interested in somebody your age who is trying to act like a young street player.

It's time somebody told you what time of day it is and I guess I'm the one. Your clock done ticked away till you almost ready for Jesus to come. It is time to sit your old hind part down. If you just got to have a woman, why don't you find a saved and committed woman of your age?" He appeared to be getting ready to say something. You could tell that he was upset, but Mother didn't let up. "Don't look at me like you going to jump me or something!

I see you swelling up like a water buffalo, but you ought to be glad, 'cause I got to tell you what the good Lord want you to know. This talk is long over due. I meant to tell you this 15 or 20 years ago, but I didn't want to hurt your feelings. I thought you'd learn some sense. There are seniors with snow on the top and fire below, but you'd never know it until they show it to the one they're with. Now you got snow on what little is left on the top and no fire below, because you can't keep a woman. How many have you had so far that didn't stay? Not only that, but you want folks to think you got it by following these young girls around. Brother Vision, don't you know these young girls will give you a stroke or a heart attack; besides an empty bank account! You think you got issues with your health now! Just wait until you mess with the wrong woman.

The Lord is tired of you taking his 'Word' and using scriptures to defile young girls. You don't want a woman your age because they can see right through you—just like I do. Walking around here talking about a woman over 40 is too old for you. What's wrong with you?" Mama was not playing and I was too happy for the message. She continued her tirade. "I ain't blind. I know you taking that Viagra and it done fooled you. You think I sit here praying and don't see and hear what is happening! You got yourself a computer and don't know how to operate it, except to meet women in that there chat room or on them sex rooms everybody seem to know about. What are you looking for in the church and on that computer?"

"What you better do is pray to God for a woman your age to help be an understanding companion to you without a lot of stress. But Naw, that's too much like right! You want a baby, old enough to be your grandchild, so you can die happy in sin! Who told you that there is a fire and where is it? You act like you are getting' ready to start World War III with all that red on. The blaze is so fiery; you'll make a blind man see. Pull some of that red off because it is too much on the eyes!"

Poor Brother Vision was so broken hearted, that you could see water glistening in his eye, but he knew better than to say anything negative. The only thing I heard him say was "Mama Edmonds, I ain't never done nothing to hurt nobody. Why you saying these mean things to me? Why you want to embarrass me in front of Reverend and Sister Nayrena 'nem?" Mother Edmonds ignored his plea and kept on talking. I told you, this woman don't play. Mother Edmonds said, "Dale Vision, God has a seat for you in the Kingdom and down here on the deacon board. You can't sit on neither one until you be a man after God's heart rather than after a woman's dress tail. You say that you are saved and filled with the Holy Ghost. If that's so, tell me why you about to lose your soul when it's time for you to cross over on the River Jordan. Your journey with the Lord started a long time ago. You and I have been through hell and high water and sometimes more than we could bear; but we made it over. I can't go back and you can't either. It is all in your mind what you think that you can do and who you think you can do it with."

"I want to see you get your reward. It is time for you to get yourself together and do better in the Lord. God is watching you and He see everything that you do. You are not too old to change. I love you despite my disappointment with you. Forgive me for saying what I believe I had to say for your sake. Go home directly after service, don't stop no where along the way, and when you get there, take off all that red. Don't ever leave your house with that much color on or they may arrest you for disturbing the peace. Now, give me a hug. Can't you see from this that a young woman can't hug like an old woman can?" Then Mother Edmonds started laughing.

I thought Brother Vision was going to be upset with her, but apparently they've known each other a long time, because he overlooked her words and laughed as hard as she did. I glanced up at him and I started laughing along with them. Pastor Sinclair had quietly escaped the melee without saying a word and chose not to get involved. Brother Vision's final response to Mother Edmonds was that people were really paying attention to him and giving him lots of compliments. He never said who the people were. If he had, it would be interesting to observe their dress and behavior. Whoever "they" were, were wrong for encouraging this old man to look like a fool on a mission. Sometimes, he makes remarks like "I'm a man of experience. I'm too hot to handle. Back in the day, I had me some fun. Today, I am thinking that with all of that red on, he truly is too hot to handle.

Chapter Eleven

"Strength and honor are her clothing: she shall rejoice in time to come." (Proverbs 31:25)

I TOLD GLENDA, EARLIER THAT I CAN'T SIT on the left side of the church anymore until the Carlyle family relocates to another church or city. If there ever was a "BeBe" set of children, they've got them. There is ten year old Jeffrey, whose hair curls without curlers and looks scary. He is tall for his age of 10, but acts like a two year old. His sister, Mary is eight years old going on twenty-five with long hair and legs that are swift to the rescue of her sibling. She has weaved hair on her head which reaches beyond her little waist and her little head is leaning from the weight. She frowns painfully from the tight braids. I would say "poor thang," but the child is so active and mouthy that you want to torture her by pulling her teeth one by one. Ouch! When you scold her, she stares intensely at you with an evil look, at least that's the way I see it. Then she calmly warns you with these words, "My mama said that she is my mama, and nobody at this church can tell me what to do. Ya'll can't make your own kids mind. How can you tell me and my big brother to shut up and be quiet when all of you are talking? If God is going to get me, he better get you all too. Leave us alone." See, I told you not to feel sorry for her. She is a fast, long-tongued, heifer. I mean that in a truthful, spiritual sense of course! Church is good for them, but they are not good for the church.

Their mama and daddy, Brother and Sister Carlyle, act like they come to church by themselves. Their off springs are laughing, talking out loud, throwing spit balls, being disrespectful to their elders, and passing licks at each other.

What is wrong with these parents who never seem to hear, see anything, and won't try to stop their children from acting up in the sanctuary or on the church ground for that matter. I know the Bible says, "Whosoever will, let them come," but this is ridiculous. These folks are beyond belief. The scripture should read "Whosoever will, let them leave." Look at Sister Carlyle, she's no beauty with that wig from the discount department store. You think I'm being mean, but it's the truth. The wig just sits at an angle, no style at all. You can see her "kitchen." The "kitchen" is a southern term for the curly, rough part of your hair on the back of your neck at the hairline. Her clothes are never really fresh looking and they always have a wrinkle or rumpled look. Matter of fact, she never looks happy. In all fairness to her, those two children probably took a lot out of her. Tired and burdened is how I would describe her demeanor. And another thing, she and Brother Carlyle don't seem to have any romantic entanglement at all. One day I over heard him tell her to "get her bad kids before they tore the church up, like they tore the house and the car up!" Other than that, you rarely hear a word from him to her or about her.

One day, before service began, Brother Carlyle finally looked up to see what was going on and rose up from his seat on the pew, but hesitated. He evidently wanted to say something to those observing his family. What he said was unexpected and humbling to both Glenda and me.

"I am sorry for my children's behavior. My wife has cancer and has been ill for a long time. She is currently in chemotherapy and has little energy to do anything. I recently lost my job and we've been struggling to make ends meet. I suppose both of us have been depressed and discouraged lately. These issues are no excuse for our negligence in disciplining our children, but I feel that I owe you all an explanation. You probably think that we are terrible parents, who don't care what our children do, although nothing could be farther from the truth.

Please accept both of our apologies and I will also personally apologize to my wife for what I said in the presence of others about our children being hers a few Sundays ago." He dropped his head and sighed out loud.

"We could stay home, but we need a Word from God to get through this terrible time of trials and tribulations on every side. We've got a lot of work to do and I hope it's not too late. We got lost in our circumstances and failed to take responsibility for our children. I feel so bad because out of frustration I have not treated my wife fairly. Please pray for us!" I sucked in my breath and exhaled slowly in regret for our rush to judgment. I was feeling so down in my spirit as I held up both hands to halt his explanation. He paused and smiled at me as I spoke, "Mr. Carlyle, I mean, Brother Carlyle, I am guilty of judging you and your family. I admit to being critical of you and your wife and how you are raising your children." He replied, somberly, "You all didn't know. We should have asked for help. We are both at fault and equally to blame. May we pray together for the needs of my family?"

Since this was the first time that I had spoken to the man I had an epiphany regarding his personality and wisdom. It was as if I was seeing him for the very first time. He had a rugged face with well defined lines of aging and his hair was sprinkled with grey; and he was probably no older than my other siblings who are in their forties.

I asked Brother Carlyle, if he would mind, if I came over sometime to pick up the children. His initial response was quiet and reluctantly he said, "If you think you can handle them, I would appreciate the help. Anytime would be fine." I informed him that the children and I could visit the cultural arts museum, see a movie or maybe attend some of the youth activities at the church. I reiterated that I wanted to help in someway, if they would allow me the opportunity.

Brother Carlyle nodded his head as if surprised at the offer, then he smiled and added, "Alright, Sister Nayrena, if you're up to the challenge." And I replied, "Trust me that has never stopped me before." We all gave them a hug and left with our own perspective about what had just been revealed.

What complicated lives we lead with all the drama we are exposed to. The Carlyle family is a prime example. What can I say? This is a hectic day. I reflect back on the many events that have taken place today and recognize that they have not all been sorrowful. As a matter of fact, some things have been humorous and some unbelievable. And to top it off, my day is still not over yet.

Chapter Twelve

"And if children, then heirs; heirs of God, and joint-heirs with Christ; if so be that we suffer with him, that we may be glorified together." (Romans 8:17).

Immediately I felt tension around me and muttered whispers. I began to observe that stares were being directed towards me. I cannot believe what is happening, not today of all days. How dare he come into my territory, my sanctuary with that woman! How dare he face me and the members of this church after what he did! At this point, I knew that I was the only one who had not seen my ex-husband on the premises, with his woman clinging to his arm. Behind me, I heard Glenda hissing like a caged reptilian creature desperate to do harm to the human being who stumbled into her cage. My ex-husband, Fred Kokomo, waved at me from across the room, and politely made his way to my side, ignoring the shocked; and yes, curious looks aimed at him. "Good afternoon Nayrena," he said, as though we were best friends. He took one of my hands in his and said, "Girl, you are still looking good." And I responded with cold hands and a numb heart, "How are you? Where is your girlfriend?" then

I added, with sarcasm, "Where are your manners? Bring her over so that I can properly meet her. The last time she was at this church, I didn't get an opportunity to know her as well as others did. We don't want her to misunderstand our conversation." Fred hesitated, but behind him, I could see her approach us, and as she got closer began to complain about being left alone. "Freddie. How come you left me alone? I want to sit down now because my feet are hurting. Are there anymore seats in that row over there by you? Come on and let's sit down!" She put emphasis on the now! She still had not recognized me.

You would have thought the stock market had crashed as the impact of her words resonated around the church. I thought to myself, afternoon service had better be on time today or we may have an "on the spot revival" or at worst, a funeral. Fred was clearing his throat and looking around at the reaction of the members. Then he faced me rather than answering his companion and paused before saying, "What can I say to the love of my life when it was me who messed up the best thing that ever happened to me? I left you bitter, hurt, with all the bills, humiliated and confused by my actions. For all of this I am sorry." As he talked, all I could think about was screaming at the top of my lungs in order to release all the pain and heartache. I needed to finally be healed. Have you ever tried to make mess go back up into the closet and it keeps falling out?

That's how I felt in this situation. If you haven't been there, don't wish for it. It is an emotional trauma of the worst kind. That's exactly what I had been doing, pushing mess back in into my emotional closet and having it fall at my feet all over again. What do you say to a man, who walked into your life, cleaned house on your cooking, wiped his feet on your kindness and stepped all over your love? A man who whispered things in your ear that you knew must be a symphony that was being played with violins especially for you? A man who smiled with you at secrets only the two of you could identify with? A man who held you in his arms and made you feel like the second coming was already descending? How could I have been so blind, so ignorant and so trusting?

"God," I said, within my spirit, "you have to help me because I am weak and so angry at this man that I want to hurt him. I want to hurt him like he hurt me, only worse. Help me Lord, to do your will and not mine. I truly thought I was over these feelings of anger."

"Nayrena," Fred whispered, "please talk to me, I am so sorry. I didn't come to say any of this, but something keeps urging me to tell you how I feel." What Fred didn't understand is that I was waiting for divine intervention before I knocked his behind dead on the floor. The old me, before baptism, and unrepentant, was ready to strap on a pistol, shoot first and forgive him later. However, God began to minister to me through the Holy Spirit. He was telling me to let go of the past and move into my victory. I heard Him speaking, just like I am talking to you, in my spirit. He said, "You've been born again and what you used to do is in the past. I have restored you, anointed you and guided you to this moment." "No weapon formed against you shall prosper has been my assurance to you." (Isaiah 54:17) He didn't hurt you, he hurt my Kingdom because he professed to represent Me. Stand on My Word and believe that what you desire is already done. You are strong and your faith will take you through this moment to reclaim your joy and self-esteem.

"This is a day of forgiveness. You have mine today, Fred," I whispered, with obedient submission, "I am so glad you came today, because it's time for you and I to move on emotionally from our relationship." I glimpsed his girlfriend, and knew that she acknowledged who I was and was looking anxiously from Fred to me, wondering what the outcome would be. I continued to share my new found wisdom with him.

"Since you left me, I harbored so much resentment and sometimes hatred for you. It is true that you did betray my trust and hurt me beyond measure. You humiliated me in front of our biological families and our spiritual church family. I never thought I would look at you and see peace and blessings instead of animosity. Initially, I was ready to do you bodily harm, but God has changed me. Just now, he restored my peace of mind and has done a new thing in my life. Today, I stand before you free for the first time in years to be all that God meant for me to be. Free to love again without comparing every other man to you. Free to walk into this church with my head up high and compassion in my heart."

He started to speak, but I shook my head and held up one hand to stop him, "Don't interrupt me! I am ready to forgive you and mean it. I am not perfect, although I am learning how to live Holy and to praise God from the depth of my soul. You brought me to Christ and for that I am eternally grateful. I know now that you didn't hurt me. You hurt God and His kingdom because you professed to be a leader who represented His Word. What happened to us wasn't even about me. It was about the enemy trying to destroy the Kingdom of God through us and we played right into His hand. Satan used us to make a mockery out of the gospel and we bought into his game. I pray that God will bless you as He is already blessing me." I heard the catch in his throat as he lamented our loss, "Nayrena, you truly are a woman of God. I thank you for helping me to unload the burden and sorrow that I've experienced for what I did to you. I messed up with you and God."

Then, before I could react, he pulled me to him and kissed one side of my cheek. I quietly said in his ear, "Don't let me go ghetto on you Negro. Release me before I take you back, and then the members here will experience a gender war right here in this church." He released me and we both smiled in total understanding and somehow, the years before ceased to exist as before with all of its pain, hurt and depression. Only God can do that for us. Did you hear what I said? Only God can give you strength, restoration and deliverance while you are still calling Him.

The people around us, watching anxiously for the explosion to occur, audibly sighed in relief, as we embraced.

His girlfriend was distraught as she moved closer to hear what we were saying. She grabbed his hand tightly as if to say, "No way, no how, not today." I was able to smile at her, and shake her hand for I no longer held animosity towards her. She did not have to fear retribution from me. I could understand her hesitancy to take my hand and I sensed an element of fear. She did not have to worry. I had been there and done that. I would never treat her as she did me. I told her as warmly as I could, "You are a blessed woman and I forgive you for what you did to my marriage. I can see that Fred is a changed man and you are evidently one of the reasons why. Hold fast to the Word of God and He will do great things in your home and spiritual lives."

She looked at me in surprise and then spontaneously hugged me with so much enthusiasm that I almost fell down. She meekly declared, "I am so glad to have your forgiveness." In my ear, privately she whispered, "Freddie and I are both so sorry for what we did. He hurt you and I was just as guilty for having an affair with a married man. I thought when he left you for me, that my guilt would lessen, but it has become worse and has created issues within our relationship. After we relocated and began to work in our new church home, our sin stood between us and true worship.

We learned that sin will not allow a person to rest without forgiveness. We had to come today in the hope that we could find peace and solace. We'd wanted to wait until service was over to meet with you, but thank you so much. You don't know what you have done for us…for me…today." She began to cry, softly "You are the blessed one, the anointed one and a virtuous woman of God. What can I say to you, but I'm sorry." Fred blew me a kiss and they walked away together to sit in a pew up front, arm and arm, happily engrossed in the knowledge that despite the past, all was well.

To the onlookers, my friends, and members of my beloved church, I could only smile to reassure them that I, too, was okay for the first time since my marriage ended. Some of you have been where I am today and you can witness that it takes God to overcome this kind of hurt.

Chapter Thirteen

"And all these blessings shall come on thee, and overtake thee, if thou shall hearken unto the voice of the Lord thy God." (Deuteronomy 28:2)

Somehow, my outlook on life was more serene and the beauty of praise and worship was much more beautiful. Members were shaking their heads in disbelief at the failed battle in the church. The underground gossip press reporters would not have a late edition for tonight's community church review. I guess it's time for the afternoon services to begin. At this point, I have no idea what time it is. Our Pastor, Rev. James Sinclair, is taking his seat in the pulpit. Pastor Sinclair is a good looking, intelligent man. I guess you say that every man in leadership is handsome and intelligent, and for the most past, you are right. I will always alert you to the ones who are...on the prayer side. Rev. Sinclair is as fine as wine at dinner time with a tip sitting on the sidelines. His wife, she's alright, but she's been beaten down by members who love to player-hate, mostly women. She is not as friendly as pastor, but she and I get along.

Some of the young women deliberately ignore her presence when pastor is around. They hike up their skirts and actually "purr" when they talk to him. I've heard them say things like "Reverend, I've made you a peach cobbler. Can you pick it up later?" Or, "Reverend, what size shirt do you wear? I saw some beautiful ones at Neimann Marcus and I must get one for you." I've also heard them say, "Reverend, I've got a problem and I need your advice. When can we meet so you can counsel me? It is so hard talking to everybody." When Pastor Sinclair acknowledges his wife and suggests a woman to woman counseling meeting or joint counseling with both of them, you can visibly see the expressions of disappointment.

A few women in question have said, "Well, that's all right Reverend. What I have to say is private and Sister Sinclair might not understand." The thing that I appreciate most about Pastor Sinclair is his sincerity and spirituality. "Sister," he will say, "my wife and I are a packaged deal and you can't have one of us without the other. Have a good day and be blessed." Let me tell you what I would say to female members who don't respect minister's wives. May I be honest and blunt in my dissertation? Here goes:

To Be A Preacher's Wife

A pastor's wife must be strong in the Lord. She has to believe that she can be all things to
the majority of people in the congregation, in spite of her treatment. She must be swift to ignore rumors which often surface in the church.
This woman of God must learn to cry on the inside and rejoice outwardly because there was never a promise

that her road would be easy. If we were to ask for a wife's testimony, these are the words she might say:

"Being a pastor's wife is not easy. I've been one for a number of years and I know the thrill of victorious living and the agony of defeat. I'm not ashamed to tell you, that it takes God in a Spirit filled home that spreads the gospel. There have been times that I've been neglected, rejected, suspected, and disrespected, while my husband was praised and projected--
Times when I had to smile in the face of adversity--
Times when I wanted to cry, but knew that I had to be strong for the sake of my mate, my children and my church.

Other women can wear what they choose, but I am constantly criticized and reminded that I am a pastor's wife. Evidently, some people feel that I need to be reminded of my role, but they fail to understand that I am first of all...a woman. I need to be loved, appreciated and told that I am beautiful. I want to be noticed just as other women. I love nice clothes and a decent home with all the rights and privileges that belong in my marriage.
When problems arise in the church and my husband is being discussed, I gain strength from the knowledge that I am there to support him. If he is wrong, behind closed doors, I must communicate the truth of God's gospel and not mine. To be a minister's wife is not to know everything, but to relate to all things. I have to be wise as

a prophet and gentle as a dove in order to love others regardless of what they do to me. So often I have been accused, abused and misused, sometimes amused, and seldom excused…but I hold my head up with pride and dignity.

It hurts to see my loved ones, my children, and my mate, hunger for acceptance. To see my husband walk the floor, praying for members and their families, is so painful to me. To see him shed tears for the faithful ones who grieve as well as those who die or are in trouble, is so sad. But, one day, I know that, I shall stand before God and affirm my thanks for all he has done for me. Then I will ask to see once again my friend, my mate, my pastor, who has stood on the solid rock with me. When we shall stand before the throne of Christ and hear Him tell His Father, "These are they who have come up the rough side of the mountain. These are the ones who have washed their robes in the blood of the lamb. My joy will be the moment that I tell my Father in heaven to welcome them home."

It is then that I shall hug my loved one and shout for joy throughout God's heaven. I know that Jesus already knows, and yet, I want to be the one to tell Him for myself, all about our trials and tribulations. Through it all, He never left us alone. "Yes," I've been a pastor's wife and "No," my living with this preacher man has not been in vain. I have not wasted my time, for up the road must be eternal victory in the name of Jesus."

Ladies, we have to keep the gospel real in our hearts. When a prophet of the Lord holds up his shield of faith, and allows you to glimpse true love and commitment, why should we become angry at the messenger? I am a witness that I have foolishly done that and had to be forgiven in the Spirit. I can say "Amen" to the pastor and his wife. After hearing her words, I believe that I will be able to understand her behavior much better. We have to help our pastor be strong in the gospel by living saved lives in his presence and outside of the House of God. When we love his wife and his family, we give honor to him as a leader. Can I get an "Amen?"

Chapter Fourteen

"For I know the thoughts that I think towards you, said the Lord, thoughts of peace, and not of evil, to give you an expected end." (Jeremiah 29:11).

TODAY THE CHOIR IS DRESSED IN THEIR new robes that are blue with gold trim. They are rocking to the tune of "What a Friend We Have in Jesus." Heaven is definitely in their view. Devotional services as we call it, is spiritually motivating and the prayer soothing to the soul. I can tell by the enthusiasm of the entire congregation that they came to have church. We have guests all the way from Chicago, Illinois. They are from The Church of Thanksgiving and Deliverance. The pastor is Reverend Richardson Mango, Jr.

The secretary has just announced that there will be a church meeting on Friday night and all members are expected to attend. I looked down at my Bible and had a private conversation with myself. "Not me," I said. "I will never attend another church meeting as long as I live. The last church meeting I went to was over 10 years ago down in Oak Ridge, Tennessee. It was like Saturday night in the Ever Ready Club. I've never seen anything like it. Deacon Smith was accused of continually parking in Pastor St. John's parking space at the church. His wife was accused of stirring up trouble by sitting in the anointed seat of 1st Lady St. John whenever she gets a chance and the 1st Lady has to sit some where else.

If that wasn't enough, the associate minister, Reverend Seagram, was accused of "shacking" up with Sister Ora Mae Defender, the Sunday School Teacher.

The members were told that 'word is out' that she was pregnant with twins, and Reverend Seagram was not divorced from his wife who was a member of the same church. One member complained that she had a financial situation a few months before the meeting, but when she came to the church to request assistance to pay several bills, she was told by the board that they had already given their quota for the year to those in need. According to her, the church finance board scrutinized her life and earnings worse than the local bank ever did. She was embarrassed because she was always a faithful tithe paying member. Her response to them was "I've never asked for anything from this church—I've always given beyond what was asked. To know that you would treat me this way is too painful to discuss. I've watched people walk in off the street and you freely give to them without question. How much do you think God loves me?"

And to make the meeting more explosive, Pastor St. John was in trouble for taking his family on a ride to Louisiana in the church van. I had a headache when I left from the screaming and the cussing. Yes, I said cussing and I believe that if a gun had been there, somebody would be dead. I left with the intent of resigning my membership.

Now, you tell me why I should attend another church meeting? The only thing missing was a bottle of scotch, a gun or a knife, a deck of cards and some down-home blues.

I know that I'm not perfect, but I cannot comprehend why Saints of God cannot get along. I came from the streets where people could care less about your feelings. Nobody prepared me for church mess and perpetual stress. I came to the House of God to be embraced in the fellowship of Believers and I found division and animosity on a whole new spiritual level. "How can this be?" I asked as a new convert. I believe that people doing right things right do not have to engage in negative and critical meetings. Jesus, himself, said to Peter. "Upon this rock I will build my church and the gates of hell shall not prevail against it." (Matthew 16:18)

However, the reality is that hell does prevail and the business of the church is not operating well for many churches. For that reason, numerous churches have fallen prey to sin and closed their doors.

Even though the accusations may have been legitimate, I believe that there were better ways to deal with the issues presented. First of all, the church should have had administrative bodies to help resolve most of these issues before they got to the floor of a church meeting. Secondly, the pastor could very easily have dealt with the parking and seat issues that concerned him and his wife. Love and appreciation have won over many disgruntled individuals be it in church or elsewhere. It seems as though some people love to come to church and fight about a gnat on the wall. Seriously, I recognize that there are issues that must be dealt within the church body, and sometimes, those issues may create dissension, but it should not be a result of gossip, hateful spirits, and favoritism. No, never again will I attend a church meeting unless God puts a flashlight on me, and tells me that He is going to chair the meeting.

I apologize for my digression, getting back to the service. Reverend Mango was also the speaker of the hour. You have to know that the man can preach you out of your seat, but his favorite topics are about sinful women and righteous men. If you can get past that, you are in for a real treat. I hear tell, that he has divorced two wives before he married the one that he has now. Of course, that's his business, but how can he really talk about some of the commandments such as, "Thou shall not commit adultery" and not be condemned himself?

My Pastor, Reverend Sinclair, is standing and the choir is through singing. He's introducing Pastor Mango and singing his praises. Reverend Sinclair is a wonderful, saved and sanctified man and I've never heard him say a mean word or do anything to hurt or harm anyone. He gives back to the church for the poor and the needy.

He has taught us to sow seeds of love and money in order that we reap what God says we can have. We have a God sent leader. He is a true man of God. What I can't understand is why he always invites Reverend Mango to our church when he knows the man's track record?

I suppose he wants to believe the best when I'm sure he knows the worst. Oh well, he's ready to begin the introductions and prepare us for the sermon, so let me get primed. "Members and friends," Pastor Sinclair, said with fervor and charisma, "it is such a privilege to introduce to some and present to others, my brother in Christ, Pastor Richardson Mango, Jr., of The Thanksgiving and Deliverance Church of Chicago. Raise your right hand to receive him and repeat with me, Reverend Mango." You had to be there to see it and hear the message for yourself. This day will go down in history. Reverend Mango stepped up to the mike and yelled, "Do you like good music? Do you like fine women? Oops, wrong words, but true for men out of bad relationships." "My text," he went on to say eloquently "is about the Bold and the Wonderful." I told you my perspective on issues in the church, so by now I was wishing I had gone home because I knew we were in for a rocky landing, especially since he took off at full speed. I closed my eyes and began to pray as he preached.

"My text today is taken from Psalm 51:5-12. Sisters, my message is in no way a reflection on your character. Today's message is about being bold in the word and wonderful in your service to the Lord. Are you listening? If you are not, you are going to miss what I am about to lay on you. This world is messed up and stressed out. We've only got a short while to do what the Lord told us to do. Everyday, I'm getting ready, packing up and putting my deposits down, so that I can ride the Amtrak Express to glory.

Are there any bold men, strong men, in the building? Do you know that many beautiful women have taken a big man down, single handedly, with no backup? Some of them are little bitty women. I know this is true because one of them took me down some years ago.

But, I prayed and drank some herbs and I got free and was delivered from that sister. David, a witness himself, prayed for forgiveness of sins, and for the right spirit, so why can't I?"

You could see the climate in the church begin to change. Nobody knew whether to say "Amen" or "Help him Jesus." He braced his arms against the pulpit podium and now he was on a roll. He continued, "Let me tell ya'll the truth. Ain't no man can take a woman of the world on and win, not if she is beautifully built like a brick house with legs like a work of art, and a voice that you imagine singing 'you make me feel like a natural woman.' You might as well throw your hands up like the police shows tell you to do during investigations and tell her, 'I give up.'

But, if you are a strong man with God on your side, you can run like Joseph did and leave your coat and everything else behind. Listen to me good. There is no temptation that can overtake you that God has not given you a way of escape. If you are alone with a good looking woman with red lipstick on and your spirit is weak, you better run like the devil is after you and never look back. If you see temptation staring you in your face and you keep staring back at it and your body gets in on the drama, brother, you are in serious trouble. Better yet, don't even go in the room alone with a single or married woman without a prayer or several witnesses. Delilah got Samson hemmed up talking about his strength and where it came from. She was bold and she was absolutely gorgeous. The sister lay down with him and Samson got so confused that he told her everything about his self and brought destruction down on him and everybody else."

"Then Jezebel, that sister was the meanest, baddest, low down, and not to mention, dirty woman, that ever was written about in the Bible. She and her husband King Ahab had a neighbor, Naboth, killed for his vineyard. She was going to kill the prophet, Isaiah too, but he ran for his life, after he prophesized her destiny. She died like he said, but she was bold, bad and wonderful. Brothers, don't be crazy. A woman is thinking while you're asleep. She will prepare you a meal that will satisfy a King. Think about a spread on the table when you are real hungry. The sister has prepared you turnip greens with smoked neck bones, fried chicken, candied yams, macaroni and cheese, fried okra, corn on the cobb, sweet country tea, and a caramel cake for dessert. She got me by the tongue. How about you brothers sitting out there today?

Cooking food that will make you moan all of your sins to her while you sleep. Many men have been killed while talking and sharing in their sleep. That's the reason I sleep soft. Do you hear me brothers?"

While he was preaching, my mind wandered again and I remembered a local news article about a criminal situation between a man and a woman. The news headline read that a woman shot a man over a bowl of spaghetti and meatballs, but I know that the food wasn't the real deal. Some of you have been in arguments with your man or your woman before, and you have to suspect like I did, that the argument was not about the bowl of spaghetti and meatballs. I believe he got smart with her and probably was abusive and the sister shot his behind. It didn't have to happen. He knew what it was about soon after she shot him. I wish I could ask him some questions. I would say, "Brother, where were you last night? Was it worth it? If you had it to do all over again, would you eat the sister's food again? Would you ask her nicely next time? Will you be quick to get smart with her? Will you pay attention next time, if she's still angry and give her some appreciation and respect? Could you say softly, "Okay baby, do you mind if I take the last of the spaghetti and meatballs?" He could have saved himself some hurt and a hospital visit.

I've got to stop digressing from the sermon and at least try to listen to Rev. Mango. I missed the majority of his message. Oh well! Pastor Mango was still on a roll as I came back to the present. He was saying, "I'm not saying all women are bad, but they can draw bad things to a man if he is out of his spiritual elements. Sometimes you don't get a second chance. God is a second chance God. Trust him better than anyone you know!

If you are married, trust your wife and wives trust your husbands. If you are single, keep your eyes and ears open. Folks have a tendency to tell you what they want you to know."

"God is getting ready to do something about sin in the world and in the church. He is tired of false prophets and back sliders, 'slipping and sliding,' their way to heaven. When God gets through with this world, it will be a burning bush waiting on a flood." He released a loud hoop and a holler. "I'll be in a ship with wings, on my way to glory. Who will go with me to that mansion in the sky? How about you Pastor Sinclair? How about you Sister Sharon and Sister Elmira? The bold and the wonderful won't have room on the boat, but they can sail on the big ship, if they clean up their hearts, study and learn obedience. All of us have to stand, but we have to know when to shut up and listen. Then he began to sing loudly, off key and out of tune, one of my favorite songs, 'Come to Jesus.'"

I tell you again, you had to be there to see the expressions on the members and visitors faces at the end of his performance. He looked pleased as punch as the other ministers placed their hands on his shoulders and praised him for the message. I, for one, knew that Pastor Sinclair was long overdue for a private conference regarding this visiting church and its pastor.

The nerve of Reverend Mango's members who shouted out of order, mind you, "Go pastor, go pastor, say it loud: preach and be proud." As they chanted in unison; they had a swaying dance routine almost like the soul train line. I kept thinking to myself, God is going to be in spiritual shock when we all come marching up to Zion with the world still determining our behavior and actions; not to mention our clothing. I think I'll fly with the birds to glory and leave the water transportation to the bold and wonderful representatives.

I know without a doubt that it is time to go home. My physical body is almost to the breaking point. Service all day from Sunday school to this afternoon's service has been an extraordinarily long day. And when you include the drama, I am definitely ready to relax at my house and in my bedroom which is my haven.

Chapter Fifteen

"I will call upon the Lord, who is worthy to be praised: so shall I be spared from mine enemies." (Psalms 18:3)

"Excuse me, were you speaking to me?" I asked and turned in time to see Sister Rita Mae Lowery rushing to my side. "Sister Nayrena, I need to speak with you," she said quickly, looking around to make sure others were not listening. I stopped and waited for her to continue. She was so agitated that her long hair kept falling forward into her face. Sister Lowery used her hands to push her hair back with an unconscious gesture. "Sister Nayrena," she said, "I'm sorry to hold you up, I really am. I need to talk to you. I have to talk to someone before I lose it. I just can't seem to feel God's spirit like everyone else. I cannot talk to anyone else about this. I don't speak in tongues or have any specific gift from God. What am I supposed to do? Am I saved or not? How do I know?" I knew that I had to be careful in my response to her questions, not to mention her trust in me as a spiritual advisor. "Sister Lowery," I replied, "you are one of the most anointed saints of this church. Everyone does not worship God in the same way. We all have diversified gifts of the spirit. And, I am especially glad of that because of the love, harmony, songs and gifts that reflect the diversity of talents we have been entrusted with by God."

"Read the scriptures: (I Corinthians 13 Chapter.) Read all of it and give thanks to God for who you are in his name." I encouraged her with a hug and reassured her that it is okay for those who feel comfortable to speak out loud their faith, for it's their way of expressing their feelings of spiritual joy. "For some it's okay that they sing and pray, it's their way. For others it's okay to run, dance, shout and jump, it's their way. Some people have a tendency to moan and groan.

Others complain and act restrained in their worship, it's their way. There are those who will lift their hands and cry in adoration, it is their way. I see that you are seeking the Lord with humility and with all of your heart. As God's plans unfold for you; His plans are not of evil, but to prosper and give you hope, and then you will do it your way (Jeremiah 29:11). You will not be ashamed to witness inwardly and outwardly of his goodness."

"God created you and equipped you with special talents and joy beyond comparison. Allow the Holy Spirit, your advocate, and instructor, to guide you and know that praise, worship and favor are yours for the asking. You please God by being in the fellowship of love with your brethren. Worship and sing God's praises with your whole heart, understanding that faith comes by hearing and hearing by the word of God, (Romans 10:17). Thank God for you, my sister. I will be praying for you." We embraced after she thanked me and I tried to hurry out of the vestibule of the sanctuary. "Lord, please help me," I prayed silently because my heart is so heavy and I am so tired spiritually and mentally. Please let me go home safely, pull off my clothing, and have a restful night of peace. But alas, it was not to be. Approaching me was yet another sister with a troubled look, heading in my direction.

"Hello Sister Jillian. I didn't see you in services today," I said, "I am so glad to see you. We've missed you." Sister Jillian Williamson was a long time parishioner of our church, who had been absent for some time. "Hello Sister Nayrena," she responded, without looking me in my eyes. She started to walk away and then said, as if having an after thought, "Can we have lunch or dinner some day soon? I could really use a friend in my life." Do you know how difficult it is to be a Christian and hear another Christian tell you how much they need a friend in their life?

I shook her hand and told her that I would be glad to have dinner with her on Thursday night and it would be my treat. We agreed to meet at the Golden Soul Food Buffet and we both exited the church vestibule at the same time. I think I would be remiss in my story telling, if I ignored Sister Jillian's recent experiences. She has been alienated by many of us in the church because she did the unthinkable. She had an affair on her husband. Hell has no fury like a woman, or so society says: but if the truth be told; a man scorned will often do worse.

Sister Jillian's husband, Samuel Roche, who shared a different last name, is a non-member of our church. He belongs to The Church of Divine Holiness here in the city. I am privy to some of their personal information, because of my work in the women's ministry division. The sadness of their situation is that she was upset about her marital issues and was counseled in confidence by a minister at large in our district's ministerial counseling department. He not only listened to her, but provided sexual healing in the form of therapy, to her at a local motel. They were observed by someone in the community, who told others of our church and they both were brought before the board for misconduct in the body of Christ. Her husband found out and asked her to leave their home. His concern, according to him, was for the reputation of his family and his church. All of their years of matrimony, which was over twenty to be exact, were discounted. He revealed her sins to all who would listen, including calling the man's wife and parents. He also told of his patience and love for a wayward wife. I guess he wanted people to believe that he was Hosea and she was Gomer. Others readily believed the accusations against her, because her own husband, poor man, had corroborated what the majority were gossiping about. The man in question, the minister of enticement; I can't ever call him Reverend again, was allowed to remain in his position despite a behind closed door meeting.

Sister Jillian was ostracized and had to give up her Bible class as well as her local, state and national convention offices. Her reputation was soiled and her name disrespected, but her attendance did not falter. She tried to remain active until the righteous saints drove her slowly away with their criticism and demeaning looks. I am guilty for not speaking up for her or reaching out to give her support and affection at one of the worst moments of her life. We judged her without waiting to understand her cry for help and compassion. We watched her come Sunday after Sunday seeking acceptance with a pained expression on her face, but determination and strength in her every movement. You could almost hear her echo Maya Angelou's "And Still I Rise," as she walked with her head up high. The whispers and negative attitudes and behaviors dogged her footsteps from the moment she entered the sanctuary.

Thank God for divine retribution, because the co-conspirator never asked for forgiveness publicly. She, on the other hand, came before the church and acknowledged her sin and took her lumps and hard knocks. After a period of reaping hurt, embarrassment and suffering, she experienced what I now know was a reconnection and a regeneration of God and His Spirit of deliverance. The omega one, the sister of failure, became a sister of restoration and renewed hope, received and born again by predestination. We watched as she grew in her professional career . We watched her as she sowed seeds of a successful harvest. She lost her mate and her home, but she was blessed with more than she lost. Her car was exchanged for a Mercedes Benz and she gave the older vehicle to one of her most vocal critics, who needed a vehicle badly. How do you like that? Sister Williamson gave to the one who drove a large nail into her spiritual reputation. The thing that impressed me most was her strength in the face of adversity.

In spite of what her husband or members of both our churches said about her in the midst of the crisis, she never said a word against her husband or about him in public. Nor did she mumble or curse ministers of the cloth and their hidden agendas. We caused her to stop coming to a church that she loved. My mind went back to the scripture in (John 8:3-11), which says:

> *"And the Scribes and the Pharisees brought unto him a woman taken in adultery in the very act." They wanted Jesus to witness that she should be stoned to death as the law commanded. They needed a reason to accuse him, but he did a new thing. Jesus stooped down and with his finger wrote on the ground as though he heard them*

not." They kept asking him and he finally stood up and said, "He that is without sin among you, let him throw the first stone." Then he stooped down again and wrote something in the sand. Those who saw it were convicted one by one, beginning with the eldest and the last, and Jesus was alone with the woman. When Jesus stood up and saw nobody but the woman, he said to her, "Where are your accusers? Did anyone of them condemn you?" "No sir" she said. Jesus said to her, "Neither do I condemn you. Go and sin no more."

Before Sister Jillian left I felt that I had to encourage her in some way. As we stood there, compassion reached out and I quietly spoke into her spirit these words:

I have been praying for you and your family. Forgive me for taking awhile to come to you as the Holy Spirit directed. So much has happened in our lives to keep us from the blessings of God, but we are stronger than the enemies of this world.

I, myself, have felt so wounded and misunderstood in this battle called Church Leadership, however, the Lord has revealed that it is not about me and it is not about you. This is not our home and we are not supposed to be here. It is only by the grace of God that we are here today. My sister in Christ, we are supposed to be defeated and alienated, torn and worn from the struggle. The enemy has a plan in his attack on our homes and our faith. We are supposed to be walking with our head down and living in misery and suffering. We are supposed to be angry and hostile because we know what the issues are. We are supposed to stop worshipping and praising God for that is the trick of the enemy. It is no accident that this situation occurred. There is a lesson to be learned and we have to ask God for His deliverance and His purpose.

Sister Jillian, you must remember that in Christ Jesus,"We are more than conquerors."(Romans 8:37). "No weapon formed against us shall prosper."(Isaiah 54:1). We have the power to take back the land (the peace of God) that has been stolen by the enemy, if we faint not. You are a wonderful woman, a friend to so many who don't necessarily understand the blessings attached to true friendship.

Your presence is missed and your seat is empty. Your point is well taken, though your method is off center. When we are hurt, the tendency is to withdraw. Let me remind you that your strength is in knowing that when you are surrounded by darkness, you can still move forward to do what you need to do for your salvation. What He has for you is for you and you did not come through your trials without the Holy Spirit speaking on your behalf. Often our time is not His time to move.

Even though you feel that you've been beaten down over and over again, you can still get up and give God your best.

There are weaker members of our congregation and despondent new converts who are depending on you, and I, to encourage and instruct them in the Lord. Let go of the negative spirits and actions of others that have limited your service. It has caused you to gain your blessings without the joy to testify and rejoice with loved ones.

This is your moment to receive a Word from the Spirit of God--A life-changing Word--that will help you in your challenge to overcome what has tried to destroy you in the midst of your glory. This is your moment to rise again and speak to the enemy (devil) that has tried to steal, kill and destroy your mission and purpose—your family relationships—and your role in the Church. Others will have to answer for their part in what has taken place in the fellowship, but remember that the battle is not even about you or your mate!

This has been another critical battle, another year of losses and defeats, of pain and sorrow, and yet, when I think of what Jesus did for us on the Cross of Calvary, I see Victory with a capital V. Don't you know that the enemy is angry because he tried to kill you and your dreams time and time again and yet, you persevered? Don't you know that your secular and spiritual gifts are so awesome that he wants to sit you down? Don't you know that when he couldn't get you one way, he went after your peace in another way?

I wanted to quit—to give up my positions in every part of the church and my goal was to do so, but the Spirit of the Lord said "Be still and let me take care of your situation--For I am the One who allowed you to grow and gave you the talent that would make room for you among those who hate you for my sake." The world could care less about us, two black, strong women members, sitting on the sidelines spitting out chewing gum and half sleep in the pew.

The problem is that they forget about our Father in Heaven who will not allow anyone to block our blessings for long. I am going to work in the church until I am called to move on. If not in a leadership role, in whatever capacity I am comfortable in. When I am called names, God will give me a new name. If I am forced out of one area, my gift will make room for me in another. This is message is for you as well. When we have had our cry, we will walk back into the arena, well-rested, and tested on this journey to glory. One day, we can look back on how many storms we have weathered and say "Amen" to what has happened in the valley.

I will always remember how she walked when she left. She had a spring in her step and was so happy about her deliverance. I'll bet that she could sing better than anybody in the choir the song: "He's An on Time God." Sister Jillian had a testimony of being in sin, being tossed to and fro in the valley, and rescued to a higher power. Her faith was built on a foundation of love and forgiveness and is still standing. Until today, I never knew that I committed a sin just as forbidden in the Word of God: that of "omission." I failed to be there as a Christian to uplift and encourage a fallen angel of the cross. A sister wounded on the battle field of life not so different from myself. A sister who harmed herself and did not blame anyone else and yet, we withheld our compassion. Self righteous saints born through the blood of Jesus and we had the nerve to judge others. If Jesus would literally come down and dare to write our names in the sand, how many of us would be able to stand? I know that after I counted up the cost of my sins, I would probably be next in line to leave after the deceitful minister of counseling.

Can I get an Amen, from some of you who are hiding your dirt under a rug, in the closet, behind the house, over at Nae Nae's house, in town and out of town? We've got to stop telling folks to clean up their houses when our house needs major scrubbing, not to mention repairs.

Chapter Sixteen

"But ye, beloved, building up yourselves on your most Holy faith, praying in the Holy Ghost, keep yourselves in the love of God, looking for the mercy of our Lord Jesus Christ into eternal life." (Jude 1:20-21).

Finally, I know you don't believe me, but I am on my way home. Somehow, even the thought of home seems so far away. I shook so many hands on my flight to my car. This sister is totally exhausted and another crisis can ruin my fragile, emotional state, such as it is. I may have to skip some future services in order to be about my heavenly Father's business in a more spiritual manner. Today, I have been drained over and over again and I can't survive on feelings and conjectures. I need a word, a revelation from my Savior. This has become a personal desire to have counsel from Him if I am going to be revived. I made it to my car as tears made their way down my face like an unending stream without direction. "Why am I crying?" I keep asking myself as the flood continued, and the Holy Spirit began to speak to me with rebuke and truth. I was absolutely powerless to turn the ignition on. This was a moment suspended in time and I could not move. I gripped the steering wheel so tightly that my hands seemed void of blood. "I'm listening Lord, I'm listening. Speak to my mind, my body and my soul. I need a word. I will accept and trust your Word. Give it to me without condiments. I'll take it without regrets, but please don't leave me without a Word from you."

"Are you sure you want the truth?" The Holy Spirit cautioned, although He was calming and soothing to my ear. "Can you handle the word that I have for you? This word will release your doubts, your fears and your long delayed gifts." "Yes Lord," I answered, "I am ready for your Word, although I know that I'm not worthy of your grace and mercy. I have been up and down on my way to your Kingdom. I have been involved in conversations that are not pleasing to you. Your love has been pure, but I have been hypocritical and sanctimonious in my service and vision to God. Your mercy has set me up for victorious outcomes. Your favor has set me at tables before blessed people. Your joy has designed a website for me on your internet of faith and great works. How can I ignore your faithfulness to me when you have been my refuge and my strength? Your name gives me peace. And your name..." The spirit of God interrupted me gently, but firmly.

"Nayrena, do you know me? Have you really studied My Word enough to recognize me when you see me?" I started to speak and the spirit admonished me to be still with words of conviction. "Are you willing to stand before atheists, agnostics and hypocrites in order to glorify my name?" I again started to speak. I wanted so badly to say, "Yes, I am." But, I was unable to get the words out. I was puzzled, because usually I have a ready answer. I understood finally that to be quiet would be my moment of divine reverence with God. The

Spirit continued to provide me with priceless pearls of wisdom including my faults.

> *"You have allowed others to determine your degree of faithfulness. There were times when you sat down when you should have stood up. There were times when you should have listened to your inner voice and remained quiet. At times when others were gossiping about a sister or brother, you joined in rather than to say, "Let's go to them and pray, not criticize and accuse." I needed you to be an instrument of peace and inclusion and you practiced with your friends exclusion, and to top it off, you justified your actions. There were times when you laughed when you should have been crying and cried when you should have been rejoicing.*
>
> *There were times when you should have given hope to those who were feeling "less than," and being treated the least of all. What say you, my sister?"*

Actually, I was at a loss for words, because the indictment against me was undeniably true. I paused to reflect on my actions of the past, and especially today, as the Sunday drama occurred throughout the day. I examined my role and confessed inwardly that I had seriously engaged in wrongful Christian ethics that were morally wrong. Few people knew my inner turmoil regarding my lack of integrity and character assassination, but the Spirit of God knew and brought me to judgment. I wanted vindication in this matter of the heart. I needed so badly to feel the warmth, the assurance, and love of God. I wanted shelter from my own issues and lack of faith. Here I was saved, sanctified, and filled with the precious blood of Jesus, but I was guilty of ignoring my Savior. As a result of my hurt, I wounded those who most needed a word of comfort—those who wanted consolation and a reason to celebrate affirmations. I am guilty by omission as well as co-mission.

There must be forgiveness for a "wretch" like me, a sinner saved by grace. A sister who neglected sisters and brothers lost in the wilderness of their twisted and complex lives. A sister, who thought to know "righteousness" and became self-righteous--A sister who looked outwardly and often failed to see the inward trials of this life snuff out the spirit of a woman or man. I see now, Holy Spirit, the faces of those I walked past in the sanctuary--Faces so insignificant because they did not belong to my clique; my sisterhood. In order to truly represent God in every area of my life, I have to live as though He is guiding my life. I have to visualize hope and be a light to those who are seeking the Lord. People deserve to know the truth about the God that we worship and serve. As a Christian: it is my obligation to be a witness. Must I dare to be the one who will boldly stand up in the face of adversity?

Am I to be sanctioned for what others are afraid to do? Why me? As I paused in my upward plea for absolution, strong in my belief and praying for positive outcome, the Holy Spirit replied. "Yes, you are right in saying that there is a reality and that some people do need to know the truth. The issue is truth by whose standards; yours, your friends, or the truth required by God? You became judge and jury for individuals by looking at their outward appearance and gossip you heard, rather than seeking Holy and divine knowledge regarding the issues.

In order to develop a sincere and honest relationship with them, you have to relate to their diversity of gifts and talents, to their stories and challenges. In doing so, you will always have access to the Savior. We, of the Trinity, are here, day and night, to provide guidance and direction to you in how to treat others even when they are wrong. Your intentions are good, but your motives are not aligned with the Word of God."

I decided that I had to plead my case with the Holy Spirit the moment I got an opportunity to speak. I presented my case, "What about the many small children who come to church without their parents? Children who may not be dressed appropriately with poor hygiene? I see boys without haircuts and little girls with their hair standing up or matted to their small heads. They come on the church bus without a meal or even some change to put in the church offering. These are the children that I pray for in the midst of my praise and worship. I try to help them with mentoring and my personal resources. You know that I am a product of their environment and while others may rush to judgment, I have to be their advocate in an often unfriendly world. I often take them to my home and give them a bath or to the local mall to purchase clothing for them. And yet, it is not just my responsibility, but that of the entire church because we recruited them and accepted them into our love and fellowship.

We have a job to do and it's not an easy one. Parents are the key, but we have the physical presence and what we do and say will determine whether they stay or go away. That's why the church has to plan activities and trips that keep the attention of the young people who may not ever go on outings with parents or vacations in the summer like other young people do. You are rebuking me and I acknowledge my part, however, the church is just as guilty as I am.

I understand that although we weep, the task of 'growing children' requires more than a tear. It requires our blessings, discipline, love and assurances even when we don't feel like it. This is bigger than one of us and smaller than we think it is when it comes to resources. We are planting seeds and the harvest expected is so much more eloquent than words can ever express."

And the Holy Spirit responded, "Victory comes from being the difference when those around you are up in arms and ready to crucify another Saint in the sanctuary of God. You have to know that this world is not your home, you are just passing through. What you do today will speak louder than what you will ever say tomorrow. It is not your responsibility to count the times you or the church responds to human need. I do the calling for service and those who are of the Lord will answer. When you get ready to participate in negativity or look down on another person, please remember where God brought you from. Be careful how you build bridges along this walk of life because there is a chance that you will have to cross over the same ones on your way through life's journey. Don't be afraid to speak your mind, but that does not mean that you have to do it anywhere and anytime. I am here to guide you into all truth, however you have to be willing to listen and obey my direction in order to have power and authority over a situation."

"But, Holy Spirit, I am trying so hard to live a saved life," I cried out in frustration. "The enemy comes in and I don't always know that he's there.

He distracts me from my purpose and my mission. How can I be a light when my connection is often drained of energy and I am powerless to ignite the vision I need to see? The politics of the church is not easy. There is often deceit and corruption and few people to address it. The dollar becomes the gospel and the gospel becomes a song or a doctrine. It's difficult to sit still when there are members who need assistance; members who pay faithfully into the church only to discover that when they go through trials and tribulations, the church is the last resource to help them."

What's wrong with a church that teaches love and fails to give love? We tell people to look in the Bible and find an answer to their problems: that there must be a reason for what has happened to them. It is no secret that there are many things that we do in the name of worship that are not Biblical, but we continue to do them in the name of tradition. Change is inevitable and we preach that fact everywhere except in the church.

We say we live by faith and yet leaders in the church depend heavily on the church finances for their every need. We talk faith, but we've learned that it is not in our substance. We go by what we see and have at our disposal. This is reality. Young girls and women are walking tall, and proudly pregnant, with baby after baby and no husband and the church says "Let us pray.". We, who are saved, don't want to discuss sex in the House of the God when sex is in the House. Young boys, old men, girls, and women are sitting in the sanctuary with red eyes and slurred speech due to illegal and legalized drugs and alcohol. We pretend that we don't see them because they may pay more and attend church regularly. No one says that we will implement a drug and alcohol dependency ministry in our church.

There are no posted signs that say that those who feel the need to attend these services are welcome to come. We have lesbians and homosexuals who attend church and they regularly hear criticism and about their illicit lifestyle. There is often little woe and consideration of the human spirit. We have preachers, deacons, and teachers of every denomination, sleeping and creeping, with sisters and brothers of the fellowship. Many people are aware of it, but choose to turn their heads and refuse to deal with the significance of it. Why are we afraid to deal with what God put in place as commandments? I believe that it is because of the charismatic gifts and talents that people possess. I can only speak for me and my lack of action in the church missionary plan of salvation. I am so sorry for what I have done to affect the Kingdom work in a critical time as this. I thank you Lord for allowing me to "come" into your presence, although you have probably been here all the time and I was too immersed in looking for you to know it. Whatever the reason, I am so grateful. I hear you saying that you are not through talking to me, for me to be patient and listen for your voice…

I will be obedient in my anointing, and my joy is almost complete as I wait in expectation. The Holy Spirit has indicated that I can speak to Him at any time, and though He may not respond immediately, He hears my request at times of distress or my blessed moments.

Chapter Seventeen

"Whom we preach, warning every man in all wisdom; that we may present every man perfect in Christ Jesus." *(Colossians 1:14)*

WHY IS IT THAT MY THOUGHTS ARE rampant with questions and theories that perplex my heart? Why is it that we seek to build bigger and better sanctuaries rather than bigger and better hearts? Every leader who prospers in a church ought to want favor and seed bearing blessings for his membership, even if it means foregoing an anniversary or a pastors' aid program. I believe that leaders would receive more for being such a blessing to others. I have a problem with people telling me not to be selfish when some of the most prolific servants of God are selfish in their leadership and material expectations. Please, Holy Spirit, help me to understand how we are to grow in Christ when the enemies of the world constantly mock and distort our image of the House of God? And to be honest, we give them reason many times for their suppositions.Help me to know your purpose, your mission and your vision, so that I may be what God desires for me despite what others do!

We love to talk Jesus and how He was crucified. We talk about how He made both male and female and how he emphasized that, "It is good that man should not dwell alone." On the other hand, many leaders have, by design, put God in a box and stated unequivocally that "there is no place in the pulpit ministry of the Church leadership for a woman." Enlightenment is reserved for topics that do not take those select male ministers out of their comfort zone. You hear comments such as "A woman can't tell me nothing!"

"God ain't called a woman to preach, teach or tell a man what to do;" and "You let a woman try to come in 'my' pulpit and see if I won't cut her down before she takes a step." Or "Sure, a woman got a place in the church. She can be in the choir, teach Sunday School for women; be in the kitchen ministry; be a secretary; and teach women in the Missionary societies. There's a lot for her to do, but she can't tell a man what to do. It ain't right; it ain't Bible."

And don't forget this one, "There are certain times of the month when a woman is not clean. You know what I mean. The pulpit, the sanctuary is a Holy place, set aside for those who are pure." And the true negative, "A woman is evil. She can't handle stress. She has a tendency to be jealous, low down and dirty when she can't get her way. It's hard to trust a woman. That's what got us put out of the Garden of Eden." We have so many erroneous beliefs about God's plan for women. So many, in fact, that a great number of women are afraid to step into their ministry; their calling from God. These women sit in the pews, frustrated and hurt by the rejection of man, and the nudging of Christ.

One day, we shall come into the true knowledge of God. We'll walk into our blessings and rejoice at our claim to salvation. What a joy to know that God can use anyone, be they male or female, and not ask an earthly man for his permission. How sad to define the power of God and create boundaries that He destroyed on the Cross of Calvary. A true woman of God does not have to stand behind a 'denied' pulpit. She does not need a title or a sacred place within the Church which denotes her calling. She has qualifications that will elevate her in the favor of God to do His will. Love is her motivator, and the power of God is her elevator. She cannot go up or down on her own. A servant leadership is her calling and her strength is based on faith and a profound belief that God is in control.

The interesting thing about the perceptions and stereotypes that some men in leadership have about women is that they do not ignore the roles of women entirely. Some of them don't have a problem engaging in illicit sexual encounters with women who are willing to be solicited. They have no reservations about a woman "telling" them what they want in a sexual way, where to meet, and when the meetings will take place. These same men will break up their homes in order to be with "someone" often in the "flock" that they are a shepherd over. So many family members and church relationships suffer as a result. But…a woman can't teach or preach to them. How sad! How demeaning to women. What has never ceased to amaze me is that we will take half stepping, hypocritical, deceitful, whorish men to lead God's people rather than a proven, spirit filled woman of God. And might I add, a woman who will not tear down a man in order to step out front.

What is a woman to do when she has received her calling from God and He specifically says to her what He has expressed to so many men? Is she to tell the Spirit of The Living God, "Leave me alone because God can only use me in the bedroom, in the kitchen and as a child-bearer of many children," or should she say; "Lord, you've made a grave mistake in coming to me; and I want you to take back what you told me to do because your man of God does not believe what you told me?" Are women to tell God that He is wrong to call them, according to the men of God? Men who categorically testify that it was He who called them into the Ministry? If God is powerless in some situations and in the case of certain people—then... why shouldn't I question Him about other assumptions and doctrines?

Is a woman supposed to live as though she has never heard the repeated calls of God and refuse to answer Him?

Perhaps, she'll do like Jonah, when he was en route to the wicked city of Nineveh. Maybe she ought to do like Jonah, the preacher, who took a left turn running from the mission given by the Word of God; was swallowed up by a whale ordained by the Almighty Savior; spewed out on land at God's command, and learned to go right; and rightly divide the Word of Truth.

Look at a strong woman of God – A woman not looking for glory or to establish a designated territory. She is a woman of God with a story – A woman with a testimony that is surrounded by the favor of a Sovereign Savior – A woman with a life of tears and fears that God was able to deliver and conquer – A woman who loves, respects, and humbles herself before God, and the elders, may not get the recognition she deserves, but that is not her purpose nor her motive. God gave her a word, a mission, empowerment, and the anointing through the power of the Holy Spirit to do His will; and she can do no less than be obedient regardless of those who oppose her.

It puzzles me that a pulpit is so sacred, however we fail to keep it sacred by the broken lives, the unrepentant spirits, the red-rimmed eyes, the cruel replies and down right lies. Sin abounds because power breeds temptation and temptation craves self gratification. Self gratification demands satisfaction and the spiral continues to envelop the unsuspecting leader of the cloth. Now, don't get me wrong. I am not speaking against pastors and spiritual leaders in general. I am speaking to those who profess to know what God has said to those, i.e. women: who have declared their calling to preach God's Word or to operate in the Ministry of Kingdom building through the Word. I love to hear men of God preach. I also recognize that many of them, the greatest and most charismatic, have their own demands, and issues that should minimize their judgmental attitudes.

When I see women in the Bible accepting their calling amidst serious, discrimination of the female gender, I shudder to think what they truly endured. I hear so often the scripture from Malachi 3:10 which begins with "Will a man rob God?" and I, in this instance am inclined to say: that He already has robbed God when he professes that there is no way that God can usher a woman to the front of the bus to sit down in a reserved seat made by hand; to preach the Word of God who brought her there in the first place. Sermons are heard all over the country with excerpts like "God can take the impossible and make it possible." And "If you have faith the size of a mustard seed, you can be blessed," and "Sarah and Abraham were old, but God caused their prayers to be fulfilled." And yet another one, "God stood on nothing and created something." And I love this one "God can use anybody to do his work." And one more for good measure, "God went into the grave and in three days He rose with all power in His hands. What a mighty God we serve." And the footnote is: Except in His role for a woman – then it seems that God is sorely limited.

Now maybe I am totally off the chart and what I believe or think I am seeing and hearing is irrelevant. All I want is clarity, understanding and consistency. Why am I debating this subject? I suppose if Sisters and Brothers in Christ are ever going to walk the streets of Glory, we've got to at least be honest with each other, and know that we can walk together. When God gives us a Word, we can't wonder about it, we have to be active and passionate in our pursuit to do His will.

I remember vividly an incident of gender discrimination at a friend's church located here in the city. Her name is Lisa Dawoo and the name of her church is The Non-Denominational Freedom Church of Christ that sits on the corner of Grand Central Boulevard and Cross Street, right in the heart of the suburbs.

I happened to be visiting their service that day and got a serious theological revelation from the church leadership. The drama began when Sister Laney May Ferguson declared in the morning worship that she had been called to preach. You would have thought Satan had come in full glory to purge the church with fire and brimstone. Everything ceased to be… including the praise and worship. This testimony certainly seemed to be out of order, even though they had asked for testimonies. A spirit came over that sanctuary like you would not believe. I have to give credit to Sister Ferguson for her humility and calmness in the face of opposition beyond belief. The pastor seemed to be having heart trouble because he clutched his chest and sweat profusely ran down his face. He angrily told Sister Ferguson before the congregation that she was wrong about her calling, and could leave the church if she didn't like the doctrine and beliefs which "his" church "would" follow. I heard later that their doctrine emphatically stated that a woman would not be allowed to preach or stand behind the sanctified pulpit of God. One of the other main reasons was that she was trying to create a problem by going against what she already knew and accepted at the time of her baptism.

There were stunned members and guests such as myself who heard the conversation. We recognized that Sister Ferguson never missed a beat as she was escorted by several deacons and appointed mothers of the church toward the exit doors leading to the lobby. As she walked out and into the vestibule, Sister Ferguson held her head high and her courage was unfailing in light of this heartfelt moment. A number of us left our seats to leave as well.

My heart was so burdened that I wanted to put my head down and cry. I didn't know her personally, but I felt her pain. I could see that others in the crowd felt the same way by their response.

She slowed down as she got closer to the door and I glimpsed tears streaming down her cheek. Sister Ferguson turned to her adversaries as she said to the Pastor, "Reverend, I must have a word to say. Will you allow me one last opportunity to speak? If not, I'll be on the outside praising God by myself." I admired the Sister as she stood her ground and refused to back down from the scrutiny of the men and even some of the women that had denied her calling. Amidst the endless chatter and whispers such as "Why she gotta preach" or "Can't she teach a missionary class or in the Sunday school?" "She just want to start trouble. I knew when she started running around town speaking on those Women Day Programs that it wouldn't be long." "Why can't she wait for our Women's Day because it was designed to have a woman speaker?" Oh, and the award winner goes to the lay minister that venomously said "If God had wanted a woman to preach and lead a man, he never would have made the man first. He would not have, over and over again, in the Bible, have referred to the man rather than the woman."

I almost went there. You know to the place where fools will often go in a conversation and forget about the consequences, but I didn't because I was a visitor. You can probably imagine what I wanted to say. I wanted to say on her behalf as well as every other woman: that if you literally interpreted the Bible; and have a tendency to use the word "he," meaning man or the God Head, there would be a serious issue. First and foremost, there would be no need for women to worship, praise and serve based on who certain portions of the Bible refer to – namely "He." It is important that I clarify for you that a man was commanded by God to lead; that God gave man dominion over all of the earth. This does not mean that a woman was not called by God to minister, to pastor and to evangelize souls into the Kingdom realm.

Getting back to the Sister in question, Sister Laney Ferguson; the sister preached in the vestibule, standing fearlessly by the door.

She had a word for those who dared to block her blessings. Her delivery was so powerful that many of the members who were leaving came back and began to say "Amen" as she spoke. I will never forget the message that she gave to the pastor and church officials that Sabbath day morning. She said, "I got up this morning feeling fine and came to "my" church to get a Word from God. This was a day that I needed more than ever to be blessed. I didn't come to acknowledge my calling like God told me to do several years ago. However, Pastor you preached a powerful message today when you preached

"Are You Willing to Sacrifice to be a Servant Leader of God?" I thought about my soul and what I need to do in order to make it to the Kingdom of God; and the Holy Spirit told me to move into my calling. That's when I witnessed my calling into the ministry; in the presence of those I love. I thought you would be happy for me. What I discovered has hurt me beyond measure.

You see, Pastor, I got up this morning with a testimony of God's love surrounding me, soothing me, and including me on His awesome journey of healing and deliverance. It was only on my arrival at "His" sanctuary of praise and worship that I felt like an unwelcome guest. The presence of the Lord is here. I know that it is because I felt it in the depth of my spirit. I moved at His command. The problem appears to be me and my name is not on the church's agenda. When I said that I have been anointed and appointed by God to minister the Word: you all went into attack mode; and no one heard anything beyond my desire for recognition of my calling. I never told any of you to give me a seat, to give me a Sunday to preach or even an Easter speech. You're so stressed and upset about my testimony and declaration of God's calling; that you will put me out rather than face the truth of "Whosoever will."

I left home early this morning because I was so excited about worship service today. I couldn't understand why I couldn't sleep and couldn't be still.

I didn't know that God was sending me on a mission before I received my revelation. On my way here today, I passed an old man walking in the cold with no coat, and no boots; and I had the opportunity and the resources to take him to an all-night Walmart Store where I dressed him so that he could be warm. Still I was restless and God showed me another Samaritan. On my way here, I saw a prostitute on the corner and I stopped and prayed with her and gave her our church brochure. She was hesitant to take it, but she promised to read it and come to service next Sunday. If I'm not mistaken, I think that was her sitting on the back row, waving at me when I was escorted from the sanctuary, but that's alright. On the way here, I saw a drug dealer, giving me a sign to buy one of his crack rocks and I stopped long enough to explain to him about the "Solid rock" called Jesus on which I stand. He listened impatiently, but he listened. One day I believe that he will be "rocking in somebody's choir" or talking to other young men about the day he was transformed while selling death and found a Savior who was giving life to those who sold out to Him. He will probably remember the woman who told Him about Jesus Christ, our Savior of the world.

On the way here, my brothers and sisters, I saw some children. Maybe some of them belonged to you. They were fighting in the street; and I stopped and pleaded with them to go home. They had bats and sticks and looked to be no more than 13 to 16 years old. Some listened and some refused. We must weep for our children and parenting must be a priority. The church has a mission to make a difference in the streets rather than to determine who is greatest in the Kingdom. I sat there in my car and cried and prayed for God to restore and reunite a disconnected people.

Still on my way here today, which is why I came late, I saw a drunken man, holding his bottle and staggering across the street, without regard to his safety.

Suddenly, I saw him fall down and he couldn't seem to get up. I tried to drive away but could not prevent myself from getting out of my car to help lift him up. Other people stopped as well to help him and together we put him back on his feet. We watched him stagger up the street, assuming that his home was nearby, or so we hoped. I thought to myself, "If only he knew about the divine water of Jesus Christ and the blood of Calvary's Cross. If only he could receive a life-changing Word on today as I am about to receive."

And yet, when I got here, you let me know that God has no power to promote me in the gospel. Laney Mae Ferguson, a mere woman, with limited gifts and diversities; according to man. I could speak to God's creations all the way here, help them and encourage them, evangelize and love them, but the church cannot accept who I am in Christ Jesus. Did they forget that a woman was the vehicle God chose to bring Christ from Heaven to an earthly mission--She was an Esther that transformed a King's word that her Jewish nation of people would be saved from death-- She was a Debra that led her people to freedom--She was a Ruth that refused to give up her love for Naomi, her mother-in-law, and found love in the barley fields of Boaz--She was the Sojourner Truth, known as Black Moses, who told the south and slavery "to let my people go" – This woman was a Rosa Parks who sat on a segregated bus and said; "I'm tired, and I'm not moving" and started a national revolution--She was my mama and your mama, who stood up in the south and told the plantation owner that "my child" is not going to pick cotton, they're going to school."

Can someone tell me why God can use a woman to satisfy a man, be the force of the church or it would sometimes be empty; but hesitate to include her in his ministry plan?

"Actually," she said, "you don't have to accept me because Christ did it already on the Cross of Calvary when He said, "Whosoever will, let them come." The Word says, "The harvest is ripe, but the laborers are few." I have faith that God will direct me to the mission most needed in the House of God. I am prepared as you've heard, to go into the hedges and the by ways to bring in the lost sheep that have gone astray, or never heard of Jesus. I am prepared, seasoned, furnace ready, denied and tried, anointed and appointed, just to be able to stand here today and witness that you, too, shall stand and give your report on willing workers of God. Despite this confusion, I must love you – I must forgive you."

And then, I saw the Woman of God look at each of them in the face, the pastor and officers of the church, and said as she stepped outside of the door, "Greater is He that is in me than he that is in the world." Then she ended her statement by saying, "Thank you Pastor, for allowing me these few words. I have loved this church for so many years and we have had great services in this place. Please remember that I bear you no animosity for what has happened. I only ask that you consult God when you come to your defining moment of truth." The response from the Pastor and leadership was to hurriedly turn around and enter the pastor's office where they shut the door for a private meeting. In the process, they refused to answer those who questioned their authority to do such as thing; not to mention the lack of respect they displayed towards a faithful sister of the church, Sister Ferguson. The word on the street was swift and open to interpretation. When the sister walked out of the door, people crowded around, clappng their hands and singing "We shall overcome someday." Some even began to shout their frustration. A number of them, like me, had tears in their eyes. How sad in times like these when there is so much suffering to see situations of this magnitude.

I heard that Rev. Laney M. Ferguson has a powerful message that daily draws men and women off the corner due to her testimony of love and forgiveness. And so, that Church among many, will continue on; crippled in its efforts to explain how God can do the impossible, but won't make change possible where women are concerned. We love to tell new converts that God can use anyone, that he has employment in the vineyards, and that the Lord needs willing workers in the faith. And that is fine, except they will learn that they are not expected to graduate from elementary service to a major role without a crisis or God's divine intervention. Maybe one day, we will believe and receive what Christ truly died for in the Gospel. Our mission must be to never give up as some of us drink from bitter cups in the sanctuary of God.

I can't understand why I have this burden on my spirit, Lord. Why am I so concerned about those in the household of faith? Why can't I go home and feel good about what I've seen and heard in the Word? What is it that you want me to do with the discernment? Here I go again with another revelation…

Did you know that there is loneliness in the Church? So many men and women burdened and stressed by the cares of this world. They are tormented by sickness, family rejection, crime, politics, and economic crises. And to top it off, receiving little encouragement spiritually that deals with realities of the present life in which they live. The loneliness is tangible and you can see it in the eyes of older Christians, in the stance of mature adults and on the faces of the children. Wealth and poverty for many has already occurred in terms of dreams and hopes. It's time for a resurrection not speculation. It is time for a re-birth of souls neglected that need to be re-directed and not dissected. Somebody needs a word, a hug, not a shrug, as if to say "Oh, well!" Some member deserves a visit, a handshake, a gift, a flower, a card and even a sermon on "There is no greater friend than Jesus in your time of suffering."

I'm ready to do what I have to do and I dare you to do the same. We are our brother's and sister's keeper. We are invested in their lives and their salvation. Loneliness is not just a single individual's dilemma. It is a predicament that married couples, singles, and others who are mentioned earlier, have faced throughout the ages. I vote that we embrace, activate, and dedicate more love, time and resources to fellowship among the lonely.

CHAPTER EIGHTEEN

"For many shall come in my name, saying I am Christ: and shall deceive many." (Matthew 24:5)

MY MIND IS DELVING BACK INTO THE past and reminding me of incidents that I had pushed aside hoping to forget. I can see them just like it was yesterday. One day, I came to the altar depressed and stressed about my financial state. I wanted so badly to be blessed even though I caused my own distress by abusing credit cards and writing checks that had insufficient funds. At the altar was an elderly woman who appeared to be prosperous. She was neatly dressed and seemingly fine until she opened her mouth for praise and worship. I almost passed out from the liquor fumes that hit me full in the face. I quickly surmised that she was drunk and not a little bit. As a matter of fact, she was so intoxicated that she had to be lifted from her knees when the prayer was over. I am sure that some members believed that she had bad knees and had difficulty getting up until they got close to her.

The deacons who assisted her had the same reaction as I did and once she was seated, I noticed that they all moved away with their nose slightly elevated. And I, a woman of God, was so critical of her for having the audacity to enter the Lord's House under the influence of alcohol. On my way to my seat, the Holy Spirit convicted me. "Except for the grace of God, there go you," I heard Him say, and startled I looked around the crowded sanctuary to see who was speaking to me. The Spirit of God spoke into my inner ear and pierced my soul. "Why did you avoid this woman who came to church looking for a refuge? You are the anointed Saint that I ordained to reach out to the misfits and the troubled when the world cast them aside.

You are looking at the outer person, but the disease, the pain that drives this condition is on the inside. Did you hug her regardless of the discomfort to you? No, you didn't. Did you whisper to her what I whisper to you in your distress that 'God loves her and so do you?' No, you didn't. Did you whisper a prayer for her deliverance? No, you didn't.

"You looked at the symptoms and ignored the treatment. Go to her before she leaves today and share with her your testimony of deliverance and how God gave you living water that was not from the well. She needs a friend, a prayer warrior, an intercessor who will not give up on her. You need an awareness that in your own family there is a need for truth during powerless situations. Open up your heart and let me guide you to your truth and understanding for successful evangelism. This is your day to receive a revelation about your true purpose in life.

"This woman is the voice of so many women and men of our time, who are addicted and afflicted, crying out in the urban wilderness of this life. She is fighting for every moment to stay clean, but is weak and vulnerable. The enemy does not teach strength and endurance. That is why you must be vigilant and steadfast in your mission to reach lost souls. If you make yourself available, I will empower you to do what must be done to truly bring lost souls to Christ. You do not have the power to save anyone, although with my help and strength, you can do what must be done. You can do all things through Christ who strengthens you." (Philippians 4:13)

After the service was over; I went over to the woman at the instruction of my spiritual encounter with the Holy Ghost and embraced her. I noticed that several other members who observed me came over and did the same thing. I wish you could have seen the woman's face even though she was inebriated. She seemed surprised by the show of affection as tears ran down her cheeks. When she left the church, she was not stumbling as she did when she came in earlier.

Several weeks later, that same woman was back visiting, and I declare before God that she was sober. This time I didn't have to be reminded to be a witness. There, I have said it. I have acknowledged and witnessed my hypocrisy and sin of omission and co-mission. I have confessed my faults regarding a sinner who needed salvation and deliverance.

Speak to my heart Lord, for there is a war going on in my spirit. Speak to my mind, so that I can disconnect my mouth and engage my wisdom. Speak to my body, so that it will come under the subjection of your will and my steps are ordered by you. I need you to speak to my emotions, so that what I'm experiencing is not only about me, but about love, appreciation and a sincere desire to make a difference in the lives of others. Oh God, I am praying for the healing of bodies, emotions, and souls. I give you all praise, dear God, for delivering me on this day.

I hear you telling me, that I'm not always in your will, because I allow others in the gospel, to impact my effectiveness as an evangelist, a friend, a prophet, a teacher and a witness.

You say that I am one thing to some and another to the rest. You say I try to be all things to all people, and that I am as far from you as the East is to the West. I hear you saying, that I am anointed, that I am your child, but I need deliverance.

You have asked me to take my hands off others, to delay my prophecies, and to stop asking you for things that I have the power to get myself. This is too heavy for me, Lord. Will you remember the good that I have done in your name--the paths that I have made for so many people in your name? The programs I have put together which brought attention to your mission and objectives? How can I take my hands off of those in need and withhold my prophecy from those whom you've given me a Word to bless?

I'm confused and anxious; please clarify for me your thoughts. I know you don't have to, but I want to know, so that I may receive my anointing and become more "God centered rather than me-centered." After a pause, the Holy Spirit commented, "My child, you have built your own little kingdom down here on earth. You do not want to rock the boat, so you sit in it and watch people go up and under the depth of their storms and you assist only if they call you, otherwise, you don't move. You have the audacity to prophesize to those that you perceive to be weak when, if you listen to me, I will show you those who appear to be strong but are weaker."

"There are many that I could show you, who need a word, but you operate outside of my will. What you say in prophecy is often beyond what I declared and only what I can deliver. You say that you lay hands on the sick, but without my name, you have no power. You must be sincere and faithful to those you serve and not just lead to your own understanding. Seek me and allow me to direct your path (Proverbs 3:5, 6.) I know where to go and what route to take. Trust me...I've gone before you, in you, behind you, beside you, through you and over you more times than you will ever know."

My emotions were tested and I was surely, obviously stressed. My biggest regret is that I closed my eyes to some issues and pounced on those of lesser importance by my own standards. I owed it to myself and others to find out more before passing judgment. After all, I've not been a Saint by any stretch of the imagination. No matter what obstacles were put in my way, I had a charge to keep and a mission to undertake--A mission of service, caring and love for those in need of a Savior. Somehow I failed, but thank God that He is a second chance God to those who ask His forgiveness.

Today, that person is me. I am the upright, respectable Christian who haven't always walked the straight and narrow. I am the one who smiled on the outside and cried in the lonely hours of the night--Me who spoke highly of people in their presence and smothered them with fire and brimstone when their backs were turned--Me, who pretended everything was okay and then stayed up all night plotting deviously how to pay somebody back for what they did to me.

Chapter Nineteen

"In whom we have redemption through His blood, even the forgiveness of sin." (Colossians 1:14)

My mind even went back to the services a few weeks ago when I and a number of members were present for a midday service. I was in an unusually critical state of mind. If you got in my way, so be it; you were the lightening rod. I was ready to lay my religion down and put your behind on the ground. Many members had already assembled when I came through the door and took my seat. I was seated in the pew with Sister Loretta Berman, Sister Lena Sparrow, but nearer the aisle with Sister Ida Mae Westover. The first members of the choir were marching in behind Pastor Sinclair. I saw Sister Ida Mae lean forward as the tallest and largest man in the choir came in. He is the charismatic Choir Director sought after by many churches in the area. His name is Larry Plantaker. Larry is tall and dark with really good hair which he wears in a long pony tail, bound by a black band of some sort. He is a good looking man to a fault, with a physique to die for.

He has a firm jaw, full lips and the most gorgeous bedroom eyes. Even I drooled at first when I met him until I learned about his deceitful ways. I became aware of Sister Ida Mae singing softly one of those old Dr. Watts hymns, "If the Lord don't help me, I can't stand the storm. When you see me crying, that's my train fare home." Then suddenly she stood up and moved toward the center aisle where the choir was marching. I tried to grab her, just before she threw herself at the astonished brother in question. Sister Sparrow and I tried to hold on to her as she caught Brother Plantaker unaware and began to beat him down to the floor. We managed to pull her up, but she was kicking and screaming all the way to the back of the church and to the nearest restroom.

All the while she was angrily struggling to go back to the sanctuary. We attempted to calm her down, as she dropped her bombshell angrily, onto our curious ears. "I loved him and I loaned him money which he never paid back. He told me that he wanted to visit his family in Chattanooga. I gave him my pay check, as well as my vacation check to hold until he got back. He told me that we were going to be married when he returned. I believed his lies. He said he also needed new clothes and shoes, so he maxed out my credit card. I just found out that he went to Mexico with Sister Starlicia and spent every dime of my money. He has ignored me every since he got back. He won't answer my calls or my knocks on his door. I am so angry that he's lucky I didn't kill him. How could I have been so crazy to believe that he was saved?"

At that moment an usher came to the door and informed us that Pastor Sinclair had left the pulpit and wanted to see all of us in his office. "Oh, my God," I thought, "how did I get mixed up in this mess?" We begged Sister Ida Mae to stop crying and to walk with dignity to the pastor's office, regardless of the onlookers. We assured the usher, that we would be there shortly and she left. About five minutes later, we entered the office and there was Pastor Sinclair sitting behind his desk with a stern expression on his face. The look was difficult to discern, although it could have been any one of these emotions: misery, sadness, anger and unbelief; that something of this magnitude had happened in the sanctuary of God. Clinging to the arm of a chair opposite him was the man in the center of the controversy, Brother Larry Plantaker, who was bleeding from numerous scratches on his face, neck and arms! He looked at Sister Ida Mae fearfully and she glared back at him with hate spewing from her tear stained eyes.

Before Pastor Sinclair could say anything, Sister Ida Mae had jumped up and over the table like an Olympic sprinter to get to Brother Larry.

The deacons were galvanized into action and blocked her before the attack. I looked over at Pastor Sinclair and he was crying, literally in tears. I saw him wiping his face on the sleeves of his robe, but the tears never seemed to ease. My compassion for human suffering motivated me to hand him my handkerchief without regard to the feminine design embroidered on it. This was no time for etiquette. I wanted to say something, anything, to get through this nightmare of a situation, but no words would come. Standing before me was a man of God ready to preach the divine Gospel to hurting members, and he needed restoration and comfort.

I, along with Sister Ida Mae, Sister Berman, Pastor Sinclair and his wife, Brother Plantaker, and several of the deacons remained in the office; while service was conducted by the assistant pastor, Reverend Carmello Daniels. Pastor Sinclair spoke first to Brother Plantaker and what he said expressed regret as well as condemnation. "Brother Plantaker," he admonished, "what you have done has set the church back one hundred degrees to the left. You have caused heartache, sin and humiliation to invade God's House of Worship. The talent you so richly possess has become an instrument of deceit and lust. Your music has been the epitome of spiritual praise and worship. How could you defile the Lord's house by taking advantage of women seeking the favor of God? You used this sister for your own gain."

Brother Plantaker had the look of a cornered animal, caught in a self inflicted trap. Gone was the haughty, proud, arrogant and boastful demeanor. Even though I often wanted to see his spirit broken, I felt somewhat sorry for the individual sitting before us.

One of the deacons, I don't know which one, angrily yelled for Pastor Sinclair to "kill the Negro and be done with it, 'cause he done had my daughter, and my sister's gal too. I say, let's beat his tail, and throw him off the premises!"

Hearing this new information, Sister Ida Mae's emotions were once again heightened and she lunged in Brother Plantaker's direction. This time she managed to get a hold of him, and she scratched him with a vengeance before they were pulled apart. Of course, he was screaming for her to stop and trying to get away; a big man like that. I never would have thought it in a million years. At the same time, the rest of us were watching and moving in slow motion at this sudden turn of events. We could not believe what was happening.

Sister Ida Mae was screaming at Brother Larry, "You dog, you used me and abused me in the name of the Lord. You told me that God told you in a vision that I would be your wife, your soul mate, and your babie's mama. Then your lying, sorry, nasty, no-good, hypocritical, Bible reading, blaspheming, knock-kneed, double dealing, deceitful, whore mongering, cheating worm; do you think you can keep on making a fool out of me? I don't think so, not anymore! Give me that shirt and pants you got on. Pull those shoes off too. They belong to me just like everything else you claim you been blessed with. Remember, the scripture "naked I came into the world and naked I will return?" You can return just like I found you, playing church like you played in the clubs. Whore hopping in the choir and the church seems to be your specialty."

"Let me tell you what you better do and this is a promise. If you see me coming from now on, you'd better be strapped brother, 'cause as God is my witness: I'll operate on you myself and take out everything that has offended me." Pastor Sinclair intervened by asking everyone to be quiet and calm down.

He reminded us to remember our calling as we softly whispered to Sister Ida Mae to sit down and listen to the pastor. Pastor Sinclair stood between the two of them with his hands stretched out, pleading for order. Then all of a sudden Pastor Sinclair exploded for lack of a better word. Due to the noise level outside of the office, he needed to get everyone's attention, because the adrenaline of everyone in the room was charged to the limit of human capacity. He said angrily, "Sister Ida Mae, you are totally out of order. I am ready to preach and cannot. Why? Because I have two so-called saints clowning, beating up on each other, and tearing up this church with your mess. How dare you bring your dirty laundry to the church and expect people to clean it for you? How dare you bring disrespect and shame into the house of the Lord! Do you know, that by the end of this service, the rumor mill will run out of here, testifying to the terrible fight that occurred here, even though most of the people saw very little?"

Brother Plantaker was wiping blood from his face. The red welts and abrasions on his arm looked like ground sausage. He kept saying over and over, "I'm sorry, I didn't mean to hurt Sister Ida Mae. Pastor, talk to her and tell her I'm sorry. Please forgive me." Sister Ida Mae told Pastor Sinclair that she was sorry for fighting in the church, but that the brother deserved it. "Pastor Sinclair," she whispered in a hoarse voice, from screaming so much. "I am sorry, but this man has taken advantage of my love and generosity. It was never my intention to bring my pain and agony to the church. You don't know what I have gone through as I watched him go from woman to woman in this" same" House of God with his lies. Over half of our choir has felt more than the 'spirit' under his direction." Pastor Sinclair listened and held his hands up for the rest of us to be quiet.

He started to speak, but Sister Ida Mae interrupted him without apology. "Pastor, I have to leave this church before I do or say something else that I may regret.

Allow me to leave with some dignity and pride, if I still have some left. You might as well revoke my membership, because as long as Brother Plantaker is here, I will not be attending. I have to leave. I feel so badly about my part in this situation. He and I both sinned through the church. I am hurting so much and yes, I brought my hurt into the church. Please forgive me." She did not wait for Pastor's response.

We watched as she opened the door and walked out with her head up, though her clothing was torn at the sleeves, rumpled, and her hair was in disarray. I felt so sad for the misery and defeat etched on her face and the manner in which she left. The anxiety of everyone in the room was obvious. The pastor and the rest of us further discussed the unfortunate incident. Sister Ida Mae had no idea that Brother Plantaker had also "hit on me." I had long ago declined the invitation and cursed him out royally. Well, I have to be honest, don't I? Prayer was the last thing I thought about in the process of dealing with his "pimping in the church behind." His gift of music and directing is awesome and nobody can take away from that.

Pastor Sinclair told Brother Plantaker that he would be taken to the hospital for a check up shortly, although afterwards he would be relieved of all his offices; and must attend counseling to remain a member at this church. He must also seek God's forgiveness as well as those he had wronged. He stated without preamble, to those in the room "I accept some of the blame; and so should you as a Board because if we are honest, we all saw what was going on and closed our eyes, as long as no one complained. Sister Ida Mae was one of our most effective witnesses and we should do all that we can to keep her membership. I had no idea that she was part of this "Pimping in the church house conspiracy" as I have just learned as a phrase associated with us. My God, My God: how much more is concealed, and is yet to be revealed during my leadership?

We must meet to reassure the membership, that all is well inspite of this incident." Pastor Sinclair went on to say, "Lust and greed in the church has killed many congregations, destroyed many great leaders, and hindered the work of Christ. God has declared in His Word, that the gates of hell will not prevail against the house of the Lord. I must be more watchful and prayerful as a Shepherd regarding the parishioners who are trusting like sheep, hungering for a daily word, so that they may be fed appropriately." He then had everyone in the room form a Circle of Faith to: in his words, "pray as we have never prayed before." As we all got on our knees, including Brother Plantaker, and looked towards heaven; we experienced a revival in the truest sense of the word. Pastor Sinclair began to pray fervently and I don't believe that there was a dry eye in the room. His prayer was,

> *"Father, this is your son calling on you in a moment of heartache; in a time of trouble. You told me that I could call on you and you would answer. Here I am, calling you while I'm weak and down in my spirit. I need you to come quickly so that You can bind up wounded spirits; and cast down every evil thing that has set out to destroy your kingdom. You are the only One who can handle this situation that we are facing today. You know all about it because you allowed it to happen, so that good would come into the lives of those involved. Right now, we can't see it, but we trust you to see us through this moment of sorrow. Reaping has been done and we are sowing in order to bring about a more righteous and prosperous harvest. We have a brother and sister in need of your healing touch. Take charge of their lives and help them to clean up what has been messed up. Help us, Oh Lord; to live better before your people. I am powerless as a man, but you have all power over heaven and earth in your hands.*
>
> *You are our Shepherd and we shall not want. Please lead us to green pastures that you have set before us and we will not forget to give you the glory. Help us to be better stewards over your church and your blessings. Mold us, broken though we are and do not allow us to be crippled in our own desires. Lead us to thy throne of Grace and*

Mercy. Restore unto us our joy so that we may delight ourselves in thee. In Your Name Lord – we claim the victory and to God be the glory. Amen.

Let me tell you…when we returned to the sanctuary and it was time to preach, Pastor Sinclair preached a message like Jesus was standing over his shoulders taking notes. The Choir: Lord have mercy, they sang like never before. Their song after the message was Donnie McClurkins's song, "We Fall Down, But We Get Up Again." Need I tell you, who was shouting all over the church… me, me, me. Brother Plantaker was not able to stay for the service. He was taken to the Methodist United Hospital in Truesdell for his injuries and, I pray…a psychological evaluation. I bet you any amount of money that from now on, he will run from every woman sitting on a church pew and in the choir. It is not funny, but that little woman, Ida Mae, whopped his britches.

Chapter Twenty

"I am the Lord your God: walk in my statues, and keep my judgements, and do them; and hallow my Sabbaths; and they shall be a sign between me and you, that ye know that I am the Lord your God." (Ezekiel 20:19-20)

Lord, please forgive me for my transgressions. Talk is cheap and now I have to reap while I pray for my soul to keep. My conscience won't let me rest. It keeps reminding me of my wrongs; like the time I judged Bradford Jonesby. I spoke to Brother Jonesby as he approached one Sunday morning when I was entering the lobby of the church. I remember saying, "It's good to see you again, Brother Jonesby. How long has it been?" All the time, I knew full well that the man had just been released from prison for sexually molesting his former girlfriend, who accused him of rape.

A heinous crime which she will relive for the rest of her life, not to mention the emotional and physical scars she endured. In my heart, I loathed this human specimen of a man, but I made myself smile in order to be polite. "Why hello, Sister Nayrena," said Mr. Jonesby. "I just wanted you to know that I found the Lord and now I know the meaning of true happiness in the Lord. He has cleansed my soul and made me whole. For the first time in years, I can sleep at night."

All I kept thinking, as he spoke, was "I wonder how the woman is sleeping," but I kept my thoughts to myself. "Praise the Lord, Mr. Jonesby," I said, hoping that he would soon leave. "I pray that everyone can sleep and be at peace, especially since so many people have suffered so much."

I could see that his face was pale and he appeared to be visibly shaken. I didn't stop at that statement, but continued to speak. "I pray that you received counseling to deal with that unclean, satanic, heart of yours. If you repent and walk in the Spirit then you won't fulfill the lust of the flesh. That's what the Word says and I believe in the Word of God." He responded as though his mouth was in pain with an abcessed tooth or something. "Sister Nayrena, I was accused of that crime, but I never said I did it! My lifestyle convicted me years ago, and I fell right into the trap by engaging in a fornicating relationship with a woman outside of God's will. Of all the people here at the church, I thought you would be the most forgiving. I didn't expect a welcoming committee, but at least give me an opportunity to live my faith. Believe me, no one can do anymore than God can to punish, and bring justice to those who refuse to change. You have a good day and I hope that you have shown more love to other sinners entering the sanctuary than you have shown to me!"

Desperate to regain my image as a sanctified believer, who cared about all people, I stopped him from leaving and apologized for my actions and words of discord. I admitted that I had spoken those words without regard to whom they offended or hurt in the process. There was only one way to atone for my negative spirit and that was honesty and humbleness. "Mr. Jonesby," I begged. "I owe you an apology for my rudeness. What can I say? I believed the rumors and what the media reported. It is not my business to determine guilt or innocence. My role as a Christian is to love you and serve you through the liberty of Christ which set you free. I had no right to create another yoke of bondage to keep you enslaved. You fell from grace just like the rest of us and only through Jesus Christ can we be redeemed."

According to the Word of God, "Those who are in Christ have crucified the flesh with it's passions and desires; if we live in the spirit, let us also walk in the spirit." (Galatians 5:24-25) Also know, that there is another word for you in (Galatians 6:1), "Bretheren, if a man is overtaken in any trespass, you who are spiritual restore such a one in a spirit of gentleness, considering yourself, lest you also be tempted." He said that he accepted my apology, though I could feel his alienation towards me. I stood there alone and bereaved after he was gone with guilt descending like a hurricane upon my wounded pride. Almost too late, I realized the golden moment to witness was lost to my vindictive self-righteousness. There was no way I could deny that I needed to kneel at the feet of Jesus and have him anoint my mind, body and spirit.

My thoughts took a flight back to reflect on one of the older deacons of my mama's home church in Tupelo, Mississippi. I never will forget his name. His name was Jedidiah H. Foster. Deacon Jedidiah H. Foster was a man of few words, but when he spoke, he brought the house down. The centurion always spoke with wisdom and power. Age was not a factor or even in the equation for he made no regrets about his statements. Sometimes I was amazed at his boldness in bringing up issues that needed to be resolved by the church and dealt with by the leadership. I believed later in my life that he had few reasons to apologize because he was honest, compassionate and prayed before he spoke or made a decision to confront someone of questionable behaviors and motives. He did not wait for someone of authority to empower him; he was empowerment without question.

I am in no way saying that he was perfect by any stretch of the imagination, but his life was not so open, chapter by chapter, that you could use it to accuse him of being a hypocrite in light of his life style. Actually, you would be hard put to find an individual who knew him in the church or in the neighborhood who could break his faith testimony down in order to expose him spiritually. Neither could you deny, decry or reply to him in anger for he stood on the Word of God.

When confusion in the church would surface between the pastor and the membership, he would quietly listen; and then raise his hand to speak peace into the situation and calm would prevail.

One time the pastor, the deacons, the administrators and one of the auxiliary leader's of the church, had issues that almost tore the foundation of the church mission apart. I was young, but I was so afraid in the meeting that Jesus was going to come down from Heaven and snatch all of us up and send us to purgatory with the devil as our welcoming committee leader. What I knew in reality was that we would not be caught up in the sweet rapture with the scene that was unfolding before me. I had always been taught that the House of God was a sacred place, therefore, this behavior and attitudes of Saints was foreign to me.

I remember Deacon Foster rising from his seat with his arms out stretched, pleading for order above the yelling and accusations. I can hear him now saying in a voice of compassion, "My sisters and my brothers, let's remember who we praise and worship. Let's not forget the trick of the enemy who wants to divide and conquer us. He wants to defeat the power of God – Defeat our victory in the face of adversity. He knows how to put things in place that become more advantageous than the pursuit of Christ. This building is just an earthly tabernacle. Our mission is to create a place of worship so that the Word of God will go forth from this Holy place into the streets, the byways, and the highways, in order to compel men to come to the Lord. How sad that we place our faith in bricks and mortar rather than hearts and souls. I know that I can leave this church based on what is happening, but I choose to fight the enemy that wants to destroy us and our church. I refuse to fight my brothers and sisters in Christ. That is one of the reasons I will be willing to give up my seat for peace sake.

The scripture tells us that "The harvest is ripe but the laborers are few." I am a laborer and I want to reap from a bountiful harvest in the physical, and come to church to reap from the bountiful harvest of the Spirit. I want to be revived and anointed in the Word of God. I don't need all of this "he said and she said" mess. Brother Pastor, my brothers and sisters, we need to come to altar to be blessed by the Lord. Drop that pride, and join hands so that we can be about our Father's business of healing and building relationships that will be fruitful to this Kingdom. We are the well, and others are seeking a place where they may come and drink--A place where they can see and find the love of God--A place where worship is not talk, but it is the walk of faith— A place where folk are more concerned with living and giving than taking and faking—A place where there is no need to constantly argue and fight about position and status.

When the membership see us on tomorrow, we will be united and strong, praying and shouting, because we have come through our valley experience still appreciating and valuing the talents that we all bring to the table. We know that there are some issues to be resolved, but in the end, they are not greater than the fellowship of the brethren. Somebody sing before we pray, "Search me Lord and if you find anything that shouldn't be, take it out and strengthen me because I want to be right and I want to be saved."

Some time later, they reflected on the fact that the pastor and members were willing to listen and follow his request. What a powerful prayer service in the midst of confusion. Afterwards, they all embraced and left the church in a spirit of unity and harmony. That goes to show you that God can use anyone to perform that which he has set out to accomplish. The significance of this piece is that love and fellowship is greater than any issue that may arise.

As for me, I still didn't like church meetings and mama allowed me to stay home from then on.

Praise God from whom all blessings flow. I have finally arrived home; my sweet home, where I am able to rest and reflect on this day of praise, worship, and drama, to the highest power. As I sit here at my table, wanting desperately to sleep and reactivate my energy cells, the Holy Spirit is nudging me with His loving presence. I hear Him calling my name ever so softly, but I know that it is my Savior. "Nayrena," he said, in a voice of authority, which brooked no argument or resistance. "I have forgiven you for your indiscretions. You have been transformed by the renewal of your mind. Do not be discouraged or afraid, because I've got your back in all things. I am your source and whatever you need will be provided. Trust me for a mate, a friend, a job, a new home, anointed children, and a true church of faith. You have been living beneath your privileges. Have you forgotten that I own everything? You can ask me for anything and I will do it (John 14:14). You can expect a miracle from any direction regardless of the laws of the land or what scientists and psychologists predict for your life."

I didn't hear anything else. I couldn't, I had to get my praise on. You should have been there. I ran around my house, anointing my windows and doors, and claimed the joy of the Lord for at least thirty minutes. Then I sat down again, no longer tired, but energized by His Words. The Holy Spirit spoke to me once again and said, "Plant your seed, Nayrena, and it will grow you a harvest that will be multiplied over and over again. Praise and worship the Lord in Spirit and in Truth. You will see answers and blessings coming to you and through you for glory and honor to others." I found myself crying and clinging to every promise. I answered without hesitating, "Thank you father for loving me. I feel so unworthy, but thank you anyway.

You have taught me in one day, what I should have known years ago. You kept me here in spite of my teaching and living on half-truths, on half-filled promises and dealing with half- saved folks--Folks with degrees, borrowing like thieves, looking for blessings to seize, from unsuspecting Christians who are down on their knees--Folks with issues bringing you tissues, and holding their rituals, while they are signing their initials. Never mind the mess, when you think you're blessed in your spiritual test, while you're dealing with less than the best, on a day of rest. You know how to give a gift, how to sift through the trash and give to those who need a sanctified lift, instead of a liquor store fifth."

The Holy Spirit had to stop me, because I was on a roll. He said, before I got my next wind, "My child, sleep now and be blessed because this has been a day out of the pages of my book of life. Rest for the battle is not over, and the victory has only been won for this day and such a time as this. Wait until you see the list of characters for next Sunday, and then you can thank me. I have humor too. Good night and sleep tight. Now, you know that "a little talk with me makes everything alright." And all I could do was smile and use the Maestro, Barry White's, words "Sho' You Right."

Additional Readings Pertaining to Leadership and Worship in the Church

Leadership in the church is crucial to the heads of departments and to the body of believers who attend on a regular basis. Often what is seen and heard has little to do with the work of the Lord. We are so busy with programs and rituals, with districts, state, national and other association requirements that we fail to meet our own church responsibilities. Leadership requires a number of things which are actually basic to any organization. It requires:

Ability to Lead

Everybody cannot lead effectively. Many people are evangelists rather than pastoral in their ministries. They may be great preachers, great teachers and yet, not counselors or business-oriented to do the daily tasks that must be done. Beyond the passion must be the skill and ability to perform the tasks beyond the spiritual.

An Obligation to Follow

True leaders know how to delegate and allow those who have been placed in department leadership roles to function independently without them micro- managing. First of all, it creates an environment of trust and takes a lot of the burdens away from the ministry. It is difficult to teach others to follow when the leader has issues with being in the background. After all, they (leader) will ultimately get the credit for whatever is accomplished in good faith.

An Understanding of Human Dynamics

In the midst of our congregations will come individuals wrestling with their own demons of addictions, weaknesses, expectations and social ills that may stifle the church unless the leader is astute in his observations and aware of the pitfalls that are ever present to delay the victory of faith. Messages are to be preached, but there will be times when you must speak to the heart rather than from a prepared sermon that will not be internalized due to the stress of life experiences. People are not on the same level which is why you have to be creative with teaching the Word of God and life applications. The greatest evangelism comes when the members become participators of the Word rather than spectators, and sinners are drawn inside the walls of the sanctuary based on their witnessing.

Listening Skills

So often ministers of the gospel want others (members in particular) to listen to them, but they have no intention of listening to others. Somehow they have a belief that God spoke to them and no one else can ever tell them anything unless it is another minister and for many, that in itself becomes suspect. God may use a child to speak to the leader, the preacher or the pastor. The Word will confirm the message if it has, in fact, been sent from God. We are Servant Leaders, and not so important that we are above listening to the needs of our people. When we fail to listen to what is stressful to our membership, we become responsible for the fallout which will surely come. To ignore what we see, hear and observe without addressing it; is suicide to our ministry. Sometimes what people do not say is louder than what we verbally hear and that is more critical. Leaders should not be afraid to meet with their members to hear concerns and most of all, to be ready to address them, even if the response has to be "no."

Value and Respect for Diversity

Diversity is an awareness of the people, places and things. It acknowledges cultural differences and similarities. It asks people to question and make changes in their behavior. Whatever their lifestyles, their issues, their geographic origins and beliefs should not be an obstacle for a leader who truly value people in general. Respect will win you a following that you did not anticipate because compassion will overcome the concerns that arise. When a leader can meet and greet individuals on almost any level and gain respect, they become a force of evangelism which few can equal.

A Divine call for Ministry

A leader in God's ministry does not call themselves into the vineyard of harvesting souls for Christ. God does the calling and the fruits of the labor will reward the bearer. When God speaks anointing and favor over your life, the devil in hell cannot recall you from your purpose. Out of all the voices that you hear, like the woman with the issue of blood, you will know His voice.

A Passion and Purpose for Service in the Community

How much do you love the Lord and want to be in the presence of his Word? When you become a Servant Leader, the congregation and the community will know that you are passionate about salvaging the human needs. Your purpose will manifest itself to accomplish that which God has designed for you to do. Be committed to service and watch positive change in every area of your ministry. Outreach is crucial to church survival and the uplifting of God's kingdom.

A Humble Heart and a Peaceful Spirit

How big is your ego? Can your heart expand to forgiveness and wisdom in moments of hurt and betrayal? Are you willing to admit when you are wrong and work to bring peace in the midst of confusion? Being humble in the face of adversity does not take any of your strength and connection with God away. When you seek peace, you open up avenues of blessings that you probably never saw while you were in the glory days of service.

A lack of Fear in Confronting Issues that Affect the Congregation, be it Individual and/or the Church as a Whole.

Any leader sent from God will undoubtedly encounter some enemy forces along the way. When you know that the Kingdom of God will be affected by behaviors, attitudes and deeds of those who are under your leadership; you must take authority to deal with the issues before they become mountains and the congregation is in the valley. The way you confront the issues will determine your success. If you are comfortable dealing with situations over the pulpit as opposed to the appropriate method given biblically, then be prepared for the mess that you make in the process. You must be fair, but bold in regards to disciplinary measures when a member is overtaken in a fault. Whether you are dealing with family, friends or lay members of the church—you must operate by the same Spirit of God. You, yourself, will be subject to dismissal if you divide and conquer to gain members on your side in disputes. When you make decisions that alienate some and promote others, you create an environment of mistrust, thereby, increasing the likelihood that hurt and anger will emerge. It is easy to get back at those you are angry with than to confront, but if you want a strong membership base to advance your cause which should be the cause of Christ, realize that people and time is valuable.

Love for the fellowship and the Word of God should be greater than the position.

Great leaders continue to look at the vision, goals and objectives to build a great ministry. They find ways to contribute to the church growth and the community outreach. They recognize that it can only be accomplished by using the diversity of gifts that exist in the church. Members are not taught to hustle for monies and favors in God's House. They learn to move through the tithes and sowing of seeds in the Spirit of the Lord. Leaders love to give and teach others the principles of sowing and reaping. Members should be taught to believe the impossible, to laugh and to mourn, and to feel free to worship in Spirit and in Truth. The church is a family of born again believers who provide support during grief, joy and appreciation, mentoring for career choices, hugs during trials and tribulations, and opportunities for enlargement of territories for ministries. Leaders recognize that generational curses may hinder the growth of those who are in their congregation. As a result, pastoral and other leaders introduce seminars and classes that nurture and challenge these members to be free of their issues in order for them to provide a new legacy for their families.

There are no perfect leaders and no perfect members and for that reason, we have to do the best we can with what we have. Churches that are God fearing and God sent are being abundantly and supernaturally blessed, therefore, we have to contend that they are somewhere in the ball park of leading responsibly. We do not have to fight one another and the various ministries in order to keep our members from church shopping, and hopping, if we are doing right things right. It is time to put accountability back into the church and integrate the Word of God into all that we do before the Master comes again and finds us unprepared.

My Sistah's got a problem too big for her to win,
And I can't help her because I'm trying to mend.
I fought life and lost and found life and stopped living,
Put there by my self-hatred and a heart that was not forgiving.
We are in this game called life struggling together,
Not realizing that we have the power to make things better.
My Sistah stands outside of her circle of influence,
All she needs is faith to strengthen her endurance.
Hold your head up my Sistah and stop denying,
That you've been crying, trying and slowly dying,
In your pain of lost love and an endless breakup,
Overcoming being beat up and tore up from the floor up.
Take my hand and hold on for this is your night,
Your season and your time to take a flight-
To the Kingdom storehouse where your gifts are stored,
And the window of Heaven will open and the gates are lowered.
It's time to live in your purpose, mission and vision,
It's time for your anointing with love, peace and wisdom.
I heard the voice and felt the nudge of the Holy Spirit within,
As He whispered softly, "Help your
Sistah and you will live again.
"She is in a battle for her body, mind and soul,
And you are the chosen vessel to help her be whole.
It is not about where she sits or a title or her career,
She needs a friend to help her out and calm the fear."
Make this weekend count in the fellowship of hope,
For all of us need to have a message of how to cope.
When I see you again my Sistah of God: will you smile?
Will you remember my strut as I walk down the aisle?
Yeah, you will and so will I… for we have to help each other out!

A Church with Issues, Tissues and Sunday Morning Rituals

The Carlyle Family – Jeffrey, Mary and parents
Adrienne Artest
Sister Sondra Davis
Rudolph Masters
Anissa Dutchmeijer
McHenry Bismotry
Ms. Thang (woman in church)
Fred Kokomo & girlfriend
Sister Sadie Terry
Brother Damon Elroy
Larry Plantaker
Brother Samuel Roche
Cherry Aims
Lena Sparrow
Sister Rita Mae Lowery
Sister Suzie Aims
Loretta Shepherd
Sister Jillian Williamson
Sister Laney May Ferguson
Brother Damon Elroy
Nayrena Kokomo
Sister Angela Janae & husband

Sister Loraine Blaine
Pastor James Sinclair & wife
Sister Renee Jamison
Grandma Edmonds
Reverend Carmello Daniels
Glenda Surrell
Sister Loretta Berman
Reverend Franklin Sandusky
Jerrod Conners
Reverend Aaron Santana
Reverend Richardson Mango, Jr.
Estella & Johnson Mahohn
Bradford Jonesby
Rudy Rutherford
Reverend Sean Jamison
Sister Ida Mae Westover
Deacon Smith

Book Club Group Discussion Questions

1. Who was Larry Plantaker, describe his personality and morals?
2. What is the name of the church that Nayrena attends?
3. Who are Nayrena's two best friends?
4. What female was very flirty in church, but would not cross the lines with her friends man?
5. What church was Reverend Sean Jamison a member of?
6. What man in the story told Sister Davis "God told me to marry you"?
7. Who cooked the nasty greens and had the nasty woman's disease?
8. Name the four dramas that happened to Nayrena at church on Sunday?
9. What two young people were kissing at church on Sunday?
10. What minister did Nayrena say couldn't preach?
11. Which mother of the church did Nayrena refer to as a great mother?
12. What decision did Pastor Sinclair make about Larry Plantaker's unchristian conduct?

13. Do you think that Ida Mae Westover decided to leave her church membership at the church?
14. What was Nayrena's response at the end of the day on Sunday?
15. Are any of you acquainted with a man like Brother Plantaker at your church?
16. What two ladies have the same illnesses?
17. What is the name of the guest church from Chicago?
18. What the name did Reverend Mango give his Sunday sermon?
19. What did Sister Rita Mae Lowery ask Nayrena?
20. What was the issue with Sister Jillian Willamson?

Personal Perspectives Regarding A Church With Issues, Tissues and Sunday Morning Rituals!

1. What was your overall opinion of the members of the "Better Than Blessed Rock Of Ages Non-Denominational Church"?
2. Indicate realities of this church and congregation that you can identify with.
3. What character in the story did you most sympathize with?
4. Which three individuals from this story would you freely discuss with others in group discussions?
5. As you read this book, are you moved to make a life change, be of service to others and or encourage those who are hurting?
6. What current event in your personal life has helped you to remove issues of negativity?
7. What similar issue do women in the 21st century face in the most traditional churches of today?

Bibliography

The Holy Bible, King James Version 1611

King, Bertha M., "I Am Who I am, A Work In Progress," Benton Harbor, MI 49022, Batson Printing, Inc., 195 Michigan Street, Benton Harbor, MI 49022

About the Author

Bertha Carson-King is a native of Benton Harbor, Michigan. She has been an educator, diversity consultant and motivational speaker for over 30 years. She holds a Master's Degree and Bachelor of Science Degree in Communications in addition to a Secondary Education Certification from Western Michigan University in Kalamazoo, Michigan.

She is co-founder of the Strong Women of Faith Breast Cancer Support Group, a student of United Christian Faith Ministries and a Christian Women's keynote speaker and workshop presenter around the country.

Bertha is President of Car-King and Associates; a consulting firm in Southwest Michigan which specializes in team building, motivational speaking, management seminars, diversity training, and parenting groups. She has been a keynote speaker for numerous colleges, schools, agencies, and healthcare organizations. Her speaking engagements have included St. Mary's College, Berrien County Health Department, the Robert Wood Johnson National Conference, the 3rd National CCN Networking Conference, the Indiana Health Association National Conference, the Indiana WIC

Conference, Sex Offense Service Volunteers, Focus on Mental Health Association, Regional Cardiac Nurses' Conference, the Benton Harbor High School 2006 Commencement Speaker, the YMCA Youth Programs, and many others.

An accident in 2000 almost took Mrs. King's life, but she has rallied to help give life to others who may feel hopeless and forsaken. Her core goals include preparing women, men and families to reach beyond what they can see to embrace the faith and knowledge that will bring them to their blessings. She recently was host of her own weekly hour long radio show "Praise and Inspiration Hour" in Benton Harbor for two and one half years. Her triumphs and tragic experiences lead her to write her first book entitled, "I Am Who I Am: A Work in Progress." Currently she is the author of two new books, "A Church with Issues, Tissues, and Sunday Morning Rituals: Worship, Revival and Survival with the Brothahs and the Sistahs," along with an urban teen book for inner city girls. "I Understand, Do You?"

Mrs. King has been married for over 40 years to Otis King, Sr. and has two daughters: Attorney Kimberly Diahann King and Tara Briana Green.

Printed in the United States
122338LV00005B/145-237/P

9 781434 330994